21: Japanese-Soviet Relations:

Interaction of Politics, Economics and National Security

THE WASHINGTON PAPERS
Volume II

21: Japanese-Soviet Relations:
Interaction of Politics, Economics and National Security

Young C. Kim

THE CENTER FOR STRATEGIC AND INTERNATIONAL STUDIES
Georgetown University, Washington, D.C.

SAGE PUBLICATIONS
Beverly Hills / London

Copyright © 1974 by
The Center for Strategic and International Studies
Georgetown University

Printed in the United States of America

4-12-83

For information address:

SAGE PUBLICATIONS, INC.
275 South Beverly Drive
Beverly Hills, California 90212

SAGE PUBLICATIONS LTD
St George's House / 44 Hatton Garden
London EC1N 8ER

International Standard Book Number 0-8039-0377-4

Library of Congress Catalog Card No. 74-27559

FIRST PRINTING

*When citing a Washington Paper, please use the proper form. Remember to cite
the series title and include the paper number. One of the two following formats
can be adapted (depending on the style manual used):*

(1) HASSNER, P. (1973) "Europe in the Age of Negotiation." The Washington
Papers, I, 8. Beverly Hills and London: Sage Pubns.

OR

(2) Hassner, Pierre. 1973. *Europe in the Age of Negotiation.* The Washington
Papers, vol. 1, no. 8. Beverly Hills and London: Sage Publications.

CONTENTS

INTRODUCTION

One of the most recent developments of the Nineteen Seventies is the growing prospect of economic and political cooperation between Japan and the Soviet Union. So young is the merging "alliance" between the two nations that its implications have hardly begun to be explored by observers of international politics.

Given the profound impact that such a partnership would have on power configurations throughout the world, it is essential to take a close look at the situation. We can begin by asking, what major factors have significantly shaped Japanese-Soviet relations in recent years? What factors will tend to facilitate a close relationship and which will present major impediments? Would an increasing Japanese-U.S. estrangement lead Japan to a significant rapprochement with the Soviet Union? What are the political implications of Japan's massive economic involvement in Siberia? In today's highly charged international context, the ramifications of a Japanese-Soviet alliance are seemingly endless.

This book is concerned with only a few selected aspects of Japanese-Soviet relations: national security, politics, and economics. Part I is devoted to delineations of interest, appraisals of threat, and strategic thinking by both sides. Emphasis is on the place of the Soviet Union in Japan's strategic planning. Part II analyzes the issue of the northern territories and a peace treaty—the most important political question affecting the general state of Japanese-Soviet relations. The respective claims of Japan and the Soviet Union to the four islands north of Hokkaido will be examined, along with developments in the territorial dispute during the period between 1956 and 1973. An analysis of the motivations underlying each country's attitudes will then be presented. In Part III we will examine the question of Japan's participation in the development of Siberia. A brief review of the Siberian development projects will be followed by an analysis of the motivations each side brings to bear on the question. Though the three questions are treated separately for analytical purposes, it should be kept in mind that they are closely interrelated and exert mutually constraining influences.

This book is not intended to be a comprehensive treatment of Japanese-Soviet relations; rather, it focuses on a few questions of fundamental importance. Its main purpose is to analyze and interpret central issues that have shaped the relationship and thus to provide a basis for future assessments.

Two kinds of data were used to prepare this work. One has been obtained in conversations between the author and policy officials and other specialists in Tokyo and Moscow. Because the issues are so sensitive, no direct attribution of sources can be made. The author is grateful to each respondent for his candor and his time.

The other data used (the collection of which constituted the bulk of the research effort) came from official publications, books, periodicals, and newspapers, both in Japanese and Russian.

SECURITY DIMENSION:
THE SOVIET UNION IN JAPAN'S STRATEGIC THINKING

The View From Moscow:
Soviet Conception of Strategic Interests[1]

From the perspective of the Soviet Union, two principal military threats are present in the Far East: China, and the U.S. military presence in Asia. The U.S.-Japan Security Treaty has been a major Soviet concern because it provides the United States with bases for conducting surveillance of Soviet and allied military activities, which could also be used for air and missile strikes. Furthermore, the bases have been and could again be used for logistic support of U.S. military operations in Asia. Japan lies athwart the Soviet exit to the Pacific Ocean and would be capable of impeding passage of the Soviet naval fleet through the straits of Soya, Tsugaru, and Tsushima. The Soviet Navy's sensitivity to these strategic passages can be readily understood.

The degree of Soviet concern over the U.S.-Japan Security Treaty appears to have been reduced as détente and an amelioration of relations have occurred between the Soviet Union on the one hand and the United States and Japan on the other. A review of Soviet publications attests to an apparent lessening of frequency and vehemence in coverage of the Security Treaty. However, the Soviets maintain their fundamental belief that the U.S.-Japan Security Treaty forms a juridicial foundation for close political, economic, and military alliance between Japan and the United States, and that it constitutes a potential military threat.

A major Soviet objective, as an intermediate goal, is to sever Japanese military ties with the United States, and, if possible, to bring about a neutral Japan. This position has been indicated in publications as well as in the Soviet position at the San Francisco Peace Conference and at the negotiations leading to the Joint Declaration of 1956.

The Soviet attitude toward Japan has undergone certain changes in recent years. In the 1950s and through the late 1960s, the Soviets tended to attribute tensions and difficulties with Japan (including the northern territorial issue) to U.S. "interference". During this period, they considered Japan to be, in effect, under the control of the United States and playing an assigned role in U.S. global strategy. In recent years, to an increasing degree, the Soviets are viewing Japan as an autonomous power, potentially capable of threatening Soviet interests. First, Japan could and might undertake the formation of a military block hostile to the Soviets. Second, Japan could assume an important military role on behalf of South Korea. Soviet sensitivity to Japan's role in Korea is consistent with its belief that Korea is a land bridge linking Japan to Asia. As the Soviets interpreted the Nixon doctrine, Japan in the Far East would be prepared and able to take over a greater share of defense, both because of its own interests and in view of its obligations to the United States.

Apart from the question of whether the views expressed in Soviet publications accurately reflect Soviet official thinking, two other aspects of Japan's military ascendancy disturb the Soviet Union: Japan's technological and economic capabilities for the development of nuclear weapons, and the expansion of Japan's armament industry as a potential "arsenal for Asia". Soviet writers rate Japan's Self Defense Forces highly in regard to modernity, mobility, and firepower. They speak of the offensive character of F-4s and the effective delivery capability of Japan's rockets and missiles. Soviet publications occasionally have displayed concern over SDF deployment in Hokkaido (45 kilometers from Sakhalin) and have referred to an SDF air exercise as "provocative".

The views publicly expressed in open literature may not accurately reflect official thinking. Soviet charges of Japanese militarism and their evaluations of Japan's current military capability are probably exaggerated. In private, the Soviets show a more sophisticated understanding, and make more realistic and accurate assessments. But, at any rate, it is not Japan's military power that causes the greatest concern for the Soviet Union. Other Japanese actions in Asia affecting Soviet interest trouble them more.

China overshadows all Soviet strategic calculations and the U.S.S.R.'s approach to Japan as well. The development of close cooperation between Japan and China with regard to mutual defense would represent a serious threat to the Soviet Union. More unfavorable still would be the development of an anti-Soviet coalition between the United States, Japan, and China, which would be viewed as posing the gravest possible threat to the Soviet Union.

The View From Tokyo:
Soviet Interests as Perceived by Japan

According to Japanese interpretations, the major Soviet political objective in Asia is the attainment of a preponderant position, especially in relation to other major powers (the United States, China, and Japan). China constitutes the major focus of Soviet policy, and the Soviets are extraordinarily sensitive to developments that enhance Chinese power. The Soviet Union is seen as seeking several objectives in Japan:[2]

(1) prevention of closer ties between Japan and China and possible Japanese support in containing China;

(2) loosening of close ties between Japan and the United States; and

(3) a closer relationship with Japan which would supercede her relations with the United States and China, or at least effect her neutrality

The Soviet Union is seen as having compelling economic motives for seeking Japanese capital and technology in its development of Siberia. In the Japanese view, the Soviet Union attaches great strategic value to Japan for several reasons:

(1) Japan could be used by a hostile power as a base for offensive operations against the Soviet Union, especially in the Maritime Provinces and Eastern Siberia;

(2) if controlled by a regime friendly to the Soviet Union, Japan would be an invaluable base for Soviet operations in Asia and the Pacific;

(3) geographically, Japan lies across the Soviet Union's eastern exit to the ocean; and

(4) the three straits of Tsushima, Tsugaru, and Soya constitute vital access routes for the Soviet Navy (Nishimura, 1969: 112-114). Soya and Tsugaru are the principal supply routes to Kamchatka and Chukot from the Maritime Provinces.

The Japanese reason that, from the Soviet perspective, it is desirable for Japan to remain militarily weak and unattached to either the United States or China, assuming that Soviet-Japanese defense cooperation is unattainable. The Soviet call for a collective security system is viewed by the Japanese as an attempt at facilitating the establishment of Soviet hegemony in Asia with the design of containing China (Chosa Geppo, 1973: 10-11; Yamada, 1972: 12-15; Chosa Geppo, 1969a: 40-41; Miyoshi, 1972: 66-71; Miyauchi, 1972: 44-49).

Japan's Conception of its Own Interests

What is the Japanese conception of their own interests vis-à-vis the Soviet Union? Japan seeks to prevent formation of any hostile coalition among the other three major powers. In particular, Japan considers the development of closer relations between China and the Soviet Union as detrimental to her interests. (Parenthetically, the Sino-Soviet dispute is expected to continue for a long time.) On the other hand, a major military conflict between her two communist neighbors is also thought to be incompatible with Japanese interests. Japan is aware that possible Japanese-Soviet rapprochement would serve as leverage against a China-U.S. coalition.

Japan considers Soviet-American relations to be in a state of peaceful coexistence, reinforced by the nuclear balance of power. The recent improvement in the relations of these two countries, symbolized by the Nixon-Brezhnev meetings, is considered consistent with Japan's interests for two reasons: it facilitates Japan's own contacts with the Soviet Union, and reduces whatever threat Japan may have visualized as coming from the latter. This is not to deny, however, that the Japanese, on occasion, may harbor some suspicion and resentment toward that coexistence. It will be recalled that the specter of Soviet-American duopoly was raised in relation to the NPT issue[3] and that American credibility with regard to nuclear protection sustained further loss by the Soviet-American agreement on the use of nuclear weapons in June 1973.

The Japanese view evolving Chinese-American relations with considerable suspicion and concern.[4] They feel vaguely that the American démarche toward China may be detrimental to Japan's interests. The first "Nixon shock" and the subsequent evolution of Kissinger's diplomacy toward China and Japan reinforced Japan's suspicion that China takes precedence over Japan in the Kissinger scheme of things (Seikai Orai, 1972: 34-45). Resentment is voiced in Tokyo over what the Japanese regard as the "Chou-Kissinger understanding" concerning the function of the U.S.-Japan Security Treaty. In his conversations with Chou, Kissinger reportedly portrayed the Security Treaty as containing Japan by preventing a military buildup and an increase in Japanese militarism.

So far as her bilateral relations with the Soviet Union are concerned, Japan considers the northern territorial problem the most important political issue. Japan is committed to seeking the return of the four islands, and this reversion requires a major improvement in overall relations. Japan shares the desire of the Soviet Union for "complete normalization", i.e., to place Japanese-Soviet relations on a treaty basis. However, the settlement of the territorial question is a prerequisite. She is also not prepared to jeopardize her close ties with the United States.

Painfully aware of her near-total dependence on imports for most essential raw materials, Japan conceives it to be in her interests to gain access to fuel and other natural resources in the Soviet Union, enabling her to diversify supply sources. However,

Japan is also cautious, foreseeing clearly the possible political implications of strengthened economic ties with the Soviet Union and, in particular, her vulnerability to possible Soviet use of this economic dependence as a lever.

Japan is convinced that her security requires the maintenance of ties with the United States as a nuclear shield. In the conventional field, also, Japan feels that she must rely on the United States, hoping it would inflict enough damage on invading forces to deter them from an all-out attack. In the meanwhile, Japan is hopeful that its military capability can be strengthened either as a deterrent or at least as a holding force until U.S. assistance arrives.

Dimensions of the Soviet Military Threat

What estimate of the Soviet military threat is made by the Japanese? The level of that threat depends, of course, on the Soviet intentions and capability as the Japanese perceive them. Soviet military force in the Far East is viewed as overwhelmingly superior to that of Japan, and capable of undertaking successful military operations against Japan. However, two major factors are seen by the Japanese as restraining hostile Soviet intentions: the Security Treaty with the United States and the intensity of the Sino-Soviet conflict (Amano, 1969: 58-65).

U.S. credibility has sustained a great diminution in recent years, and there is considerable concern about the ready availability of U.S. assistance. Considerable skepticism exists regarding U.S. determination and the political feasibility of armed aid. Moreover, U.S. forces could conceivably be preoccupied elsewhere at the time of Japan's need.

The level of Japan's apprehension is partially a function of her overall bilateral relations with the Soviet Union. Specific issues, actions, and reactions affect the dynamics of mutual understanding; for example, the frequency of Soviet seizure of Japanese fishing boats near the disputed islands, and the treatment given fishermen, have a bearing on this issue. So do the frequency, location, and type of military maneuvers. The Japanese have noted with concern the increasing level in the activities of the Soviet armed forces near Japan. For example, the maneuvers of Soviet naval units take place not only in the areas of Okhotsk and Kamchatka, but in the vicinity of Taiwan and the South China Sea as well. In addition, there are missile firings and bombing exercises in the Sea of Japan and in the waters near the Soviet maritime provinces, and extensive oceanographic research is conducted in the waters surrounding Japan.

Other actions include: flights by Soviet aircraft in the vicinity of Japan's air space (estimated since 1965 at a few hundred per year), presumably to gather intelligence data about Japan's air defense system and the movements of the 7th Fleet and to protect Soviet vessels; Soviet army maneuvers, including an amphibious landing at Sakhalin from the Maritime Provinces through the Soya Strait; and general "shows of strength", notably the naval maneuvers of April 1970 (OKEAN) (Chosa Geppo, 1972: 70-75), demonstrating the might of the Soviet navy and the vulnerability of Japan.

Several external factors may condition Japan's appraisal of the level of Soviet threat:

(1) the severing of security ties with the United States or a significant estrangement of that country's relations with Japan;

(2) a decisive shift, in favor of the Soviet Union, of the nuclear balance between the United States and the U.S.S.R.;

(3) radical and sudden improvement or deterioration of Sino-Soviet relations;

(4) the development of major tensions between the United States and the Soviet Union or between the United States and China, either on a bilateral issue or on issues involving a third country (i.e., the Middle East situation or another Korean war).

The following "internal" factors also would have some impact on Japan's policies: major political and economic instability—this situation could be precipitated by a left-wing rebellion or a right-wing coup d'état, which might or might not be accompanied by an explicit external military threat; major strategic Japanese decisions, i.e., to develop nuclear weapons, to enter into a military alliance with China, or to intervene militarily in Korea.

Apart from Soviet capability, what of Japan's interpretations of Soviet intent? At present, the Japanese do not profess to see any inclination on the part of the U.S.S.R. to initiate a military attack, but by examining Japanese scenarios, we can determine the circumstances that might change this Japanese reading of Soviet intentions.

The probability of a large-scale armed invasion of Japan is considered negligible because of such factors as the overall military balance between East and West, the Sino-Soviet conflict, and, in particular, the U.S.–Japan Security Treaty. Armed attacks of limited scope are considered unlikely, though not impossible, and their probability would be enhanced by a major internal rebellion (1) supported by foreign personnel and equipment supplied from outside by air or sea, either openly or clandestinely; (2) supported by a demonstration of force on the high seas adjacent to Japan, a more explicit military threat, or the actual use of force (i.e., disturbances in fishing and coastal navigation); or (3) accompanied by serious disruption of sea transportation (Sekino, 1971: 37-49, 1970: 35-49).

An internal rebellion could occur prior to, concurrent with, or subsequent to, the disruption of sea lanes. If sea transportation of fuel and raw materials to Japan is seriously interrupted by hostile forces (Soviet submarines), Japan would be faced with severe economic dislocation, social unrest, and political crisis (Asahi Shimbun Anzen Hosho Mondai Chosa Kai, 1967a: 52-54). Suspension of overland and inland sea traffic and thermal power generation would lead to the suspension of industrial operations. Unemployment, shortages of daily necessities, food riots, and other forms of social unrest would ensue. A reduction in the morale and the capability of the SDF would occur. The possibility of the establishment of a procommunist "government" would be enhanced. The Security Treaty would then be abrogated and the Soviet Union would be invited to render military assistance. Military incursion by the Soviet Union would precede the establishment of a pro-Soviet regime and occur simultaneously with the commencement of attacks on Japanese vessels.

Japanese strategists feel that Japan's capacity to cope with such situations is limited. Several considerations sustain this assessment:

(1) the ambiguities and uncertainties of U.S. military involvement. The U.S. obligation to defend Japan is legally restricted to areas under Japanese administration; hostile action against Japanese vessels on the high seas would be excluded. Assuming the continued superiority of the U.S. military in Asia, there is the contingency that U.S. forces might be fully engaged elsewhere, making assistance difficult. Under these conditions, the Security Treaty might not be effective, either as a deterrent or as a measure for countering actual attacks;

(2) lack of effective Japanese weapons systems, such as surface-to-surface and air-to-surface missiles; and

(3) political and legal constraints impeding the effectiveness of the Self-Defense Forces.

Japan's defense strategy presupposes the timely availability of U.S. assistance. The SDF feels it must minimally insure that military attacks on Japan could be resisted until U.S. assistance arrived, so that the United States would not be confronted with a fait accompli—the establishment of a communist government and the presence of Soviet military forces claiming to be present at the invitation of the Japanese.

Japan's Conception of Its Defense Requirements

This section focuses more specifically on the conception of defense requirements held by Japanese officials and influential strategists. It examines the Japanese evaluation of their own military capabilities, the adequacy of Japan's current defense efforts, the future direction of those efforts, and possible plans for increasing the capability of the SDF.

Japan's military establishment is divided into Ground SDF, Air SDF, and Maritime SDF. These will be discussed in turn, incorporating comments on the strategic thinking, capabilities, and vulnerabilities of each branch.

The Ground Self-Defense Forces. Strategic thinking discounts the likelihood of a large-scale armed invasion of Japan in the near future (Amano, 1969: 57-97; Asahi Shimbun Anzen Hosho Mondai Chosa Kai, 1967a: 42-52). Armed attacks of limited scope are generally considered of slight probability although they are not entirely ruled out. Such attacks, however, are considered most likely to occur in conjunction with a major internal crisis involving armed revolt within Japan.

The GSDF is thus charged with the dual missions of dealing not only with direct invasion but also with internal rebellion. As the GSDF sees it, the near future would call for an internal security goal, with the objective of countering direct invasion acquiring greater relevance and emphasis in the long-range period.

A fundamental disagreement exists among the three services regarding the relative weight to be given to each service. According to the Navy and Air Force, given the country's elongated insular geography and its proximity to the Asian mainland, air and naval power ought to be strengthened so as to destroy enemies before they reach Japan proper. In response, the Army position is that a large-scale invasion is unlikely; more probable is direct aggression occurring simultaneously with indirect aggression, and therefore the basis of defense is the maintenance of internal security. This Army viewpoint is vulnerable in that its emphasis on internal security makes it difficult to justify the demands for modernization of arms and equipment beyond small arms. The Army position, however, does note that speedy and sizable U.S. assistance could be expected only in the form of naval and air power, and that the army after all is the final defense. Additionally, increased GSDF strength would serve as a deterrent to invasion.

As of July 1973, total authorized GSDF strength was 180,000 men. There were 12 infantry divisions, 1 mechanized division, 1 airborne brigade and 1 artillery brigade (International Institute for Strategic Studies, 1974: 52).

It is important to emphasize at this point that Japanese leaders are not contemplating an increase in the present force level of the army. Defense officials as well as political leaders feel strongly that a plateau has been reached and that the maximum authorized ceiling of 180,000 will remain for a long period. Japanese officials see an army manpower increase as neither necessary nor possible. They have no plans or preparations for deployment abroad of a contingent in any capacity. Defense officials are sincerely convinced that it is now and would be increasingly difficult to recruit enough men to meet an increased force level, given the sharply decreasing number of eligible young men. The number of males in the 18-24 age group, which began to decline in 1956, is expected to continue to decrease through 1975.

This problem of eligible manpower is intensified by industry's demand on this same labor force, arising from continuous economic growth. This is borne out by data and projections of population growth and demand on that segment of the labor pool with a middle- and high-school education. However, a few comments are in order. First, the number of present GSDF vacancies is not due entirely to the difficulty of recruitment. The Finance Ministry has in fact annually set the upper limit through budgetary control. Secondly, there are several measures, largely financial in nature, that the Japanese government could take to attract more recruits, but it has not actively done so. All this is not to deny the real difficulties in recruitment.

In Japan there are some who advocate greater emphasis on the buildup of the GSDF and who advocate the notion of a one-million-man local defense corps. These supporters constitute an insignificant minority. Japan's unwillingness to increase its GSDF level is also related to her judgment of defense requirements. Japan's conception of defense confines itself exclusively to her own defense, entertaining no thought of Japanese involvement overseas. Moreover, this concept of defense requirements, even for Japan alone, has been conditioned by the estimate of the availability of U.S. military assistance.

As defense officials see it, the GSDF's major weaknesses lie in two areas; these are the problems on which defense officials have recently placed emphasis and that will continue to claim priority. The two areas are mobility, particularly airborne, and local air defense capability, especially against low-altitude aircraft. Other areas requiring attention are identified as "light combat capability", and research and development. The development of missiles, especially SSMs for coastal defense, or new tank models, and of electronic warfare equipment, are identified among such research and development items.

The Air Self-Defense Forces. The second of Japan's military branches, in terms of size, is the ASDF (Amano, 1969: 137-175; Asahi Shimbun Anzen Hoshyo Mondai Chosa Kai, 1967a: 61-70).

The fundamental factor shaping the strategic thinking of the ASDF is a constitutional limitation. Authoritative statements by the Japanese government over the years have made it clear that Japan cannot under its Constitution possess "offensive" weapons. Long-range bombers and long-range missiles are specifically cited as offensive weapons. The Constitution is also interpreted as banning, except under circumstances of extreme emergency, attacks on enemy bases. This fundamental constraint has led to the development of a strategy under which Japan assumes the responsibility of defensive operations while relying on the United States for offensive operations. Implementation of the Nixon Doctrine has been viewed as leading to a situation where the time required for introduction of U.S. assistance would be delayed. Therefore the ASDF feels that its capability should be raised so as to sustain the air defense of Japan for a period of, perhaps 48 to 72 hours. More than in the other services, ASDF planners perceived the impact of the Nixon Doctrine on Japan's defense requirements and consequently showed a sense of urgency about the problem.

ASDF officials are acutely aware of the vulnerability of existing radar sites and air bases, particularly to ECM, and the need for additional airfields in the Northeast has been mentioned. Special emphasis is given to SAM defense around the major industrial centers of Tokyo, Osaka, Nagoya, and Kita Kyushu. ASDF personnel feel that the installation of BADGE, together with SAM, has enhanced mobility in deployment of aircraft. In view of the inadequacy of the BADGE system when activated against low-altitude attacking planes, there is a recognized need for the development of an airborne early-warning radar system along the Japan Sea. There is also particular concern regarding the enemy's ASM capability.

ASDF officials do not view the People's Republic of China as posing any threat to Japan proper, although Okinawa is conceded to be within range of China's planes. They do feel that perhaps in a few years Chinese nuclear development and missile capabilities will need to be considered seriously by Japan's defense planners. As in the previously mentioned case of GSDF planners, ASDF planners consider that all-out attacks on Japan are unlikely but that Soviet air attacks on a limited scale over Hokkaido are conceivable if a revolutionary crisis occurs in Japan or if there is escalation from another Korean War.

As of July 1973, total strength was 44,600 men, with about 800 aircraft, including 386 combat aircraft (International Institute for Strategic Studies, 1974: 52). ASDF officials feel that the level of total capability they ought to have today under the present circumstances could not be realized until the end of the Fifth Defense Plan, i.e., in early 1980. As for the research and development program, ASDF will place special emphasis on AEW planes, ECM, ECCM, and missiles.

The Maritime Self-Defense Forces. The third defense arm in Japan is the MSDF (Amano, 1969: 137-175; Asahi Shimbun Anzen Hosho Mondai Chosa Kai, 1967: 52-61). MSDF personnel share the views of the other services regarding the likely forms that a military threat to Japan might take. The possibility of all-out attack on Japan is discounted in view of the Security Treaty with the United States; rather, the danger of so-called indirect aggression on the eve of a major socioeconomic or political crisis would be caused or preceded by attacks on Japanese vessels by hostile submarines. This view is based on an awareness of Japan's high degree of dependence on secure sea-lanes for the continuous flow of oil and other raw materials indispendable to her economy.

MSDF planners are deeply concerned with the vulnerability of sea routes to submarine attack and mines. Therefore, readily identified as military threats to Japan are the following: mine warfare, medium-range bombers, and Soviet submarines. For the latter two, Japanese planners say they must look to the United States for countermeasures. The major emphasis of the MSDF now and in the future will be on antisubmarine and antimine warfare. Even in the area of antisubmarine warfare (ASW), the present constitutional and political constraints—which these planners deplore—make Japan look to the United States for retaliatory action against the enemy's submarine bases. For MSDF planners, the major source of threat is from the Soviet Union. The Chinese naval capability is discounted, although the planners mention that the southwest sea routes are within the range of Chinese aircraft. Of truly vital strategic importance are three straits: Soya, Tsugaru, and, most important of all, Korea (Tsushima) Strait. Blockade of these three straits, which would be made necessary by a national emergency, and which if successful, would have a decisive impact on Soviet submarine activities, poses technical problems and would not be wholly effective. The Japanese defense planners' view is that such a blockade would help safeguard the Seventh Fleet and Pacific trade routes and would prevent attacks on the Marianas, Hawaii, and the continental United States.

Most defense planners agree that the MSDF should be strengthened both in quantity and quality, but there is no consensus on the desired size of the MSDF in terms of tonnage and men. Outside of government officialdom but within the elite sector there is considerable debate regarding such questions as how far Japanese-protected sea-lanes should extend and how such protection should be attempted. Defense officials, including those of the MSDF, unanimously and strongly reject the idea of providing protection as far as the Malacca Strait. They consider it reasonable and desirable to extend the perimeter eventually to the Philippine Islands in the case of the Southwest route and eastward to Guam in the case of the Pacific route. Safe routes beyond these points would require dependence on the U.S. Navy and the cooperation of friendly countries. These officials do not think the U.S. Seventh Fleet is capable of providing security to Japanese shipping via the Southwest route and therefore feel they must rely on diplomatic means to safeguard sea-lanes in the area beyond the point halfway to the Equator. According to their estimates, Japan might be able to provide such protection westward to Okinawa and to Ogasawara on the east by the end of the Fourth Defense Plan.

In the light of the above, it is not surprising that MSDF equipment and research and development reflect the priority given to ASW. The problem of detecting submarines commands the interest of MSDF. As of July 1973, its total authorized strength was 41,400 men with approximately 190 vessels, including 13 submarines, 28 destroyers, 14 destroyer escorts/ frigates, 1 SAM destroyer with Tartar, 20 submarine chasers, 42 coastal minesweepers and others (International Institute for Strategic Studies, 1974: 52). The naval air component had about 110 combat aircraft and 60 helicopters.

MSDF planners consider the present levels of force and equipment quite inadequate and estimate the necessary and desirable level to be 500,000 tons and about 500 ASW patrol fixed-wing planes and helicopters. As a realistic goal, defense officials in charge of planning are thinking in terms of approximately 170 vessels with tonnage of around 200,000 by the end of the Fourth Defense Plan.

Maritime planners are conscious of the difficulties encountered in conducting ASW owing to such technological advances since World War II as nuclear propulsion, ECM, low-frequency, high-power sonar, hydrophone array passive sonar, acoustic homing torpedoes, missiles, and computers. Likewise, reconnaissance satellites could plot Japanese convoy and HUK positions of interest to submarines. An ASW plane equipped with high-power radar could not be expected to detect ECM-equipped submarines or SSN. Sono-buoy capability is limited to local areas where submarines exist. The sweep rate of magnetic airborne detectors (MAD) may be small despite the high speed of the plane, while ships and helicopters may have small sweep rates due to their low detection speed.

Countermeasures advocated by naval strategists include the use of a chain of islands from the main island southward as a long-range, effective sonar base. Modern sonar technology and knowledge of sound propagation are expected to lead to the development of a low-frequency, high-power active sonar capable of detection to a maximum range of 200 miles. Japan's naval strategists hope that this kind of early warning network would enable island-based planes and helicopters and HUK groups to cope with enemy submarines (Sekino, 1971: 37-49).

The MSDF's priority in research and development during the Fourth Defense Plan will be SSM, a straits defense system, intelligence-gathering equipment such as sonar, a new command and control system, and land-based fixed-wing aircraft for anti-submarine warfare. Truly independent capability would require aircraft carriers and nuclear submarines. The MSDF would need at least two to three aircraft carrier task groups, which would require the expenditure of several billion yen for the purchase of vessels and planes, plus 5400 men.

Transcending the questions of weapons systems or quantity and quality of personnel, the fundamental weakness of the SDF is evidenced in the remarkable absence of legislation necessary for the SDF operations in the case of emergency. For example, there is no legislation governing the requisition power of the government. This reflects the political climate in which defense planners must operate.

Aside from a generally optimistic or relaxed attitude toward the situation in the 1970s, defense officials and analysts accept as a matter of stern reality the powerful political constraints under which they operate. Despite noisy protestation to the contrary outside the circle of policy-makers, questions involving nuclear armaments, overseas deployment of SDF units, and military assistance to or security arrangements with Asian countries, are neither meaningful nor considered within the realm of possibility during the coming decade.

Defense planners are still wholly or exclusively concerned with the problem of self-defense for Japan. These planners are certainly aware that developments in other Asian countries such as the Koreas and Taiwan could affect the security of Japan. However, they assume that no major changes will occur in the political status of these countries, and certainly they would not or could not contribute, save economically, to the security of these countries. The question of assistance toward safeguarding the security of other Asian countries is not uppermost in the minds of Japanese defense officials. In recent years, these officials have been a bit more willing to consider the security problems of Southeast Asian nations, and are more sensitive to these problems than previously. However, the domestic constraints referred to earlier are still accepted largely as given. Any change in this attitude, if it were to occur, must come from the political leadership. Political leaders whose principle of political survival and action is that of "prudentialism" (avoidance of controversy) are not expected to provide leadership in the matter where elite public opinion and opposition political forces are perceived by the government to be solidly behind these constraints.

POLITICAL DIMENSION:
THE TERRITORIAL DISPUTE

Of all the major factors that have shaped Japanese-Soviet relations, none is more fundamental and intractable than the territorial dispute, or in Japanese terminology "the northern territorial issue". Ever since the Soviets occupied the four islands in question at the end of World War II and subsequently incorporated them into Soviet territory, this dispute has significantly and consistently affected relations between the two countries.

The territorial issue will be examined on four principal grounds:

(1) the bases of Japan's claim to the islands;

(2) the position of the U.S. government on the question;

(3) the Soviet government's stand; and

(4) a brief review of developments in the dispute during the period 1956-1973.

The major motivations and considerations underlying the respective positions of Japan and the Soviet Union will then be analyzed.

Before Japan's claim is examined, a few introductory notes on the islands are in order. The Japanese use the term Northern Territories (*Hoppo Ryodo*) in two ways. In the broad sense, the term refers to all the territories north and northeast of Japan proper that were under Japanese sovereignty before World War II, encompassing southern Sakhalin (Karafuto) south of 50 N. latitude, the entire Kurile island chain, Shikotan, and the Habomais off Hokkaido. In the narrow sense of the term, Northern Territories refers to the southern Kuriles (comprising Etorofu and

Kunashiri) and Shikotan and the Habomais. The official claim of the Japanese government has been confined to the Northern Territories in the second sense, i.e., the Habomais, Shikotan, Kunashiri, and Etorofu. Unless specified otherwise, "Northern Territories" as used hereafter will refer to these four islands.

The Kuriles make up a chain of islands, approximately 750 miles long, aligned in a north-northeasterly direction from Hokkaido toward Kamchatka. The Habomais are a cluster of small islands that, together with the island of Shikotan, are in the immediate vicinity of the Nosappu Cape in eastern Hokkaido. The total area of the *entire* Kuriles is 9,958 sq. km. The total land area of the Northern Territories is about 4,996 sq. km., about twice the area of Okinawa. The land area of Etorofu is 3,139 sq. km.; of Kunashiri, 1,500 sq. km.; of Shikotan, 255 sq. km., and of the Habomai group of islets, about 102 sq. km. The prewar population of the Northern Territories was approximately 16,500—mainly fishermen, hunters, and agricultural workers. During the summer over 10,000 were employed in the fishing industry. The "northern Kuriles" had about 170 residents and approximately 15,000 workers during the fishing season. The "central Kuriles" had 140 residents (Japanese Ministry of Foreign Affairs, 1970: 6; Noto, 1971: 8-15).[5]

Bases of Japanese Claims to the Northern Territories

The principal basis for Japan's claim to the Northern Territories is that these islands have always been Japanese territory and have never been under the jurisdiction of any other state; moreover, that Russia has always recognized the southern Kuriles as Japanese territory. In support of this contention, Japan cites two treaties with Czarist Russia: the Shimoda Treaty (1855) and the Treaty of St. Petersburg (1875).

Article 2 of the Shimoda Treaty (The Russo-Japanese Treaty of Commerce, Navigation, and Delimitation) specifies that the boundary between Russia and Japan in the Kuriles stretches between the islands of Etorofu and Uruppu. From Uruppu northward, the other islands of the Kuriles would belong to Russia, while Etorofu and Kunashiri would be recognized as Japanese territory. The island of Sakhalin was to remain, as in the past, a joint possession of Russia and Japan, since a mutually acceptable boundary could not be agreed upon. Under this treaty, the ports of Shimoda, Hakodate, and Nagasaki were opened to the Russians, and the same commercial terms existed as those offered to the United States in the Treaty of Kanagawa (1854) (Harrison, 1953: 165-174).

Under Article 1 of the Treaty of St. Petersburg (the Kuriles-Sakhalin Exchange Treaty), Japan ceded to Russia a part of Sakhalin so that the boundary between the two countries would thereafter be La Perouse Strait (Soya Strait). Under Article 2, in exchange for the above concession, Russia ceded to Japan the Kuriled Islands. The names of the islands ceded were specifically listed in the treaty, with Shumshu to Uruppu included, all lying north of Etorofu and Kunashiri (Harrison, 1953: 171-174). The provisions of the two treaties are clear evidence to the Japanese that Etorofu and Kunashiri (along with Habomai and Shikotan, which are considered to be part of Hokkaido) have never belonged to any other country and that they are Japan's *inherent* territory. The status of Sakhalin was to undergo another change. Following the Russo-Japanese War (1904-1905), the southern half of that island was placed under Japanese sovereignty by the terms of the Treaty of Portsmouth.

As will be shown later, the Soviet claim to the Northern Territories is based primarily on wartime agreements among the allies and on the San Francisco Treaty of 1951. One of Japan's arguments is that she was not a party to the Yalta Agreement and hence is not bound by it. The Yalta Agreement states in part:

> The former rights of Russia violated by the treacherous attack of Japan in 1904 shall be restored, viz:
>
> (a) the southern part of Sakhalin, as well as the islands adjacent to it, shall be returned to the Soviet Union . . .
>
> The Kurile Islands shall be handed back to the Soviet Union.

According to the Japanese view, under international law no country can dispose of the land of a third country without the latter's consent. Hence, the Yalta Agreement cannot be interpreted as having transferred Japan's sovereignty over southern Sakhalin and the Kuriles to the Soviet Union. Moreover, Soviet participation in the Yalta Agreement itself contravenes the Neutrality Pact between Japan and the Soviet Union, which assures the protection of territorial integrity and nonaggression (Nampo Doho Engo Kai, 1966: 151). That pact was to remain valid until April 1946. The Yalta Agreement was a document that merely specified the Allies' common objectives, not an international agreement formally determining the dispc tion of the territories. In either case, Japan's argument runs, she was not a party to it. Japan further points out that the Yalta Agreement was not mentioned in the Potsdam Proclamation, the terms of which Japan accepted at the time of surrender. The Soviet Union, therefore, cannot make claims on the basis of that agreement (Nampo Doho Engo Kai, 1966: 163-167).

In the Potsdam Proclamation, no reference is made to southern Sakhalin or the Kurile islands. Article 8 of the Proclamation (issued on July 26, 1945, by the United States, Great Britain, and China, and later acceded to by the Soviet Union on August 8, 1945) states that the terms of the Cairo Declaration shall be carried out and Japanese sovereignty shall be limited to the four main islands and "such minor islands" as the signatories would determine. Japan accepted the Potsdam Proclamation, and in the Instrument of Surrender (September 2, 1945) pledged to "faithfully implement the terms of the Potsdam Proclamation". The Cairo Declaration (November 27, 1943) set forth the principle of territorial nonexpansion and stipulated several changes in Japanese territories: "Japan shall be stripped of all the islands in the Pacific which she has seized or occupied since the beginning of the first world war in 1914, and all the territories Japan has stolen from the Chinese . . . shall be restored to the Republic of China. Japan will also be expelled from all other territories which she has taken by violence and greed." The Japanese argue that these were the only territorial changes in the interests of the Allied powers and that no others were contemplated. They interpret the Proclamation as not intended to deprive Japan of those areas it had not forcefully taken "by violence and greed" (Japanese Foreign Ministry, 1970: 15; Sugiyama, 1972: 23; Ballis, 1964: 42). From the Japanese perspective, the Soviet Union is violating the principle of territorial nonexpansion through its continued occupation of the Northern Territories.

The question here is whether the areas left under Japanese sovereignty in the Potsdam Proclamation correspond to the areas not taken away from Japan by the Cairo Declaration. The Proclamation is clear on the four main islands but leaves the rest of the minor islands to be decided upon by the Allied powers. It is the Japanese contention that such a disposition has not been made and that the Proclamation should be interpreted in such a way as not to contravene the Cairo principle of territorial nonexpansion (Sugiyama, 1972: 23).

Japan also holds that the San Francisco Treaty of 1951 provides no legal basis for Soviet control over the Northern Territories. Article 2, Paragraph C of the treaty reads:

> Japan renounces all right, title, and claim to the Kurile Islands and to that portion of Sakhalin and the islands adjacent to it over which Japan acquired sovereignty as a consequence of the Treaty of Portsmouth of September 5, 1905.

Japan concedes that it renounced all claim to the Kurile Islands and south Sakhalin, insisting, however, that the treaty specified neither to whom these areas belong nor the geographic limits of the Kurile Islands (Sugiyama, 1972: 26-27).

Concerning the absence of a beneficiary, the Japanese point out that the Soviet government attempted in vain during the course of treaty negotiations to stipulate that these islands be placed under Soviet sovereignty, and this failure was one of the major reasons for her refusal to sign the San Francisco treaty. The Japanese point to Article 25 of the treaty, which stipulates that it "shall not confer any right, titles or benefits" on any state unless it is a signatory to the treaty; and that no right, title, or interest of Japan can be deemed diminished or prejudiced by any provision of the treaty in favor of another state (Sugiyama, 1972: 26-27). Hence a rhetorical question is asked by the Japanese: "How did the territorial problem that remained undetermined by the San Francisco treaty come suddenly to be resolved in favor of the Soviets?"

At the time of the peace conference in San Francisco, Japan informed the U.S. government that the Habomais and Shikotan were part of Hokkaido, and that since Etorofu and Kunashiri were geographically, zoologically, and botanically distinct from the rest of the Kuriles, they should be excluded from the scope of Article 2 of the proposed treaty. U.S. Secretary of State John Foster Dulles, however, was not willing to entertain amendments to the draft treaty on the grounds that they would cause undesirable delay (Murthy, 1964: 296-297; Matsumoto, 1970: 5). With regard to geographic delineations of the Kuriles, the only explicit exclusion at the peace conference was the Habomais. Dulles stated that the term "Kuriles" mentioned in Article 2(c) did not include the Habomai Islands.

In his speech on September 7, 1951, Yoshida, Japanese plenipotentiary, rejected the Soviet contention that the Kuriles and south Sakhalin had been acquired by Japan through aggression. He referred to the absence of any objection to Japan's sovereignty over Etorofu and Kunashiri by Czarist Russia at the time of the "opening" of the country in 1855 and stated that Shikotan and Habomai are a part of Hokkaido (Nampo Doho Engo Kai, 1966: 113-114).

It is important to bear in mind at this point that evidence indicates the Japanese negotiators did, in fact, know that the Kuriles they were renouncing under the terms of the peace treaty comprised the *entire* Kuriles, including Etorofu and Kunashiri. At the Diet committee sessions deliberating the San Francisco treaty, a formal and authoritative reply was given by a Japanese government official to the effect that the scope of the Kuriles in the treaty included both the northern and southern Kuriles (Etorofu and Kunashiri) (Chosa Geppo, 1969b: 65). It is only since 1955 that Japan has taken the position that the Kuriles renounced under Article 2 do not include the southern Kuriles. The Japanese argue that Gromyko himself stated at the peace conference that several territorial problems must be settled in the peace treaty.

The Joint Declaration of 1956 and the Gromyko-Matsumoto memorandum were cited by Japan to support its position that the territorial issue had not been resolved and that the Soviet Union pledged in 1956 to hold further negotiations on the Northern Territories. Negotiations for a peace treaty between Japan and the Soviet Union began in June 1955 and continued intermittently until October 1956, when the Joint Declaration was signed. In August 1955, the Soviet Union offered to return the Habomais and Shikotan, and thus met what was then the minimum Japanese demand (Hellmann, 1969: 35). Although the Japanese delegate originally had been authorized to accept this offer, Japan persisted in demanding the return of Etorofu and Kunashiri and took the position that a final determination of southern Sakhalin and the Kuriles be made at an international conference. The talks were discontinued in late August 1955.

Negotiations were resumed in January 1956, only to be interrupted again in March 1956 by a deadlock on the territorial problem. When they resumed a third time on July 31, 1956, the sole unresolved question was the territorial one. While the Japanese position remained fixed on the southern Kuriles, it showed some flexibility on the question of southern Sakhalin and the northern Kuriles. However, the Soviet Union would cede only Habomai and Shikotan, and the talks were called off once more.

In his letter to Bulganin on September 11, 1956, Prime Minister Ichiro Hatoyama stated that "on the condition that negotiations on the territorial problem be resumed at a later date", Japan would negotiate only if it received written Soviet consent on the following five points (Matsumoto, 1966: 201):

(1) termination of the state of war between the two countries;

(2) establishment of embassies in each other's countries;

(3) immediate repatriation of (Japanese) detainees;

(4) entry into force of the fishery agreement;

(5) Soviet support for Japan's membership in the United Nations.

In his reply of September 13, 1956, Bulganin stated that the Soviet government was prepared to resume negotiations on the "normalization of relations", without concluding a peace treaty, and accepted the five points. However, since the reply made no specific reference to the territorial issue, Matsumoto was dispatched to Moscow to obtain clarification (Matsumoto, 1966: 203-204). On September 29, Matsumoto and Gromyko, then the First Deputy Foreign Minister, exchanged notes. Matsumoto's note indicated "the understanding of the Japanese Government that negotiations on the conclusion of a peace treaty *inclusive of territorial problems* be continued even after resumption of normal diplomatic relations between the two countries," and asked for confirmation that the soviet government had the same intention. Gromyko's reply stated that the Soviet government understood the view of the Japanese government and would continue negotiations concerning the peace treaty, including the territorial problem, after the resumption of normal diplomatic relations between the two countries. With this pledge secured, Japanese Prime Minister Hatoyama arrived in Moscow on October 12 for talks with Soviet leaders, and as a result the Japanese-Soviet Joint Declaration was signed on October 19, 1956.

Paragraph 9 of the Declaration states that after restoration of normal diplomatic relations, the two governments intend to continue negotiations on the conclusion of a peace treaty, and that the Soviet union agrees to transfer the Habomais and Shikotan to Japan once a peace treaty is concluded. But it makes no explicit reference to an intention on both sides to continue negotiations on the territorial problem, despite the fact that such references were included in the draft communiqués of the two countries drawn up on October 15 and 16 and in speeches delivered by both Bulganin and Hatoyama on October 15 (Matsumoto, 1966: 105-215).

The Japanese draft contains a sentence about the transfer of Habomai and Shikotan (without having to await the conclusion of a peace treaty), while the Soviet draft refers only to the territorial issue, but not to Habomai and Shikotan specifically. During negotiations on the wording of the communiqué, conducted from October 13 to 18 mainly by Kono, Minister of Agriculture and an influential party leader, and Khrushchev, then General Secretary of the Communist Party, the Japanese aide apparently chose to accept the explicit provision concerning the transfer of Habomai and Shikotan in return for dropping the reference to the territorial problem. Although Kono suggested that the Soviet Union consider transferring Etorofu and Kunashiri when the United States returned Okinawa and Ogasawara to Japan, Khrushchev responded instead that he was prepared to write into the communiqué Soviet consent to transfer Habomai and Shikotan when Okinawa and Ogasawara were returned. When asked again about Etorofu and Kunashiri, Khrushchev indicated on October 16 that the Soviet position was final. Bulganin also told Hatoyama that Khrushchev's statement on the territorial issue was final and put it in writing in a letter to Hatoyama dated October 19. This letter said "we have given Japan her choice, and no other concessions will be made" (Matsumoto, 1966: 217).

From the Soviet perspective, the territorial problem was settled and the issue was to be closed with the transfer of the specified islands, but the Japanese took exception to this stand on a number of grounds:

(1) the existence of the Matsumoto-Gromyko notes;

(2) Matsumoto's understanding that the notes and Paragraph 9 of the Joint Declaration formed an integral whole (Matsumoto, 1970: 8-9), and that there would be future negotiations on the territorial issue since the problems normally included in a peace treaty were resolved through the Joint Declaration;

(3) the fact that the issue of Etorofu and Kunashiri was the primary cause of a breakdown in peace treaty talks; and

(4) the fact that the Japanese interpretation is consistent with the only possible implication of Paragraph 9 of the Joint Declaration. Otherwise, there would have been no logical reason for agreeing to continue negotiations toward concluding a peace treaty (Japanese Ministry of Foreign Affairs, 1970: 20), and a peace treaty presupposed the settlement of the territorial question (Chosa Geppo, 1969b: 72). To the Japanese, Paragraph 9 refers to the territorial question in substance.

After his return to Tokyo, Prime Minister Hatoyama, responding to a question at a Diet committee, said that both Japan and the Soviet Union understood that there would be continued discussions on the territorial problem, including Etorofu and Kunashiri (Hoppo Ryodo Fukki Kisei Domei, 1967: 86). Japan and the Soviet Union had already agreed upon this point before his departure for Moscow. While he was in Moscow, as it happened, the return of Habomai and Shikotan was to be stipulated in the communiqué but the Soviet Union insisted on the deletion of the phrase "territorial problem", and was adamant on this point. Whether or not specified in the communiqué, Hatoyama thought the intention was clear enough in view of the circumstances surrounding the Joint Declaration. He did not consider it necessary to have a special written promise (Hoppo Ryodo Fukki Kisei Domei, 1967: 86).

Kono stated before a Diet committee that he talked with Khrushchev four times in negotiating the wording of Paragraph 9, and they had jointly decided to delete the clause on the territorial problem since he thought the intention clear enough, in view of the following (Hoppo Ryodo Kisei Domei, 1967: 86):

(1) opinions on both sides had been clearly expressed;

(2) negotiations had been conducted following agreements between Hatoyama-Bulganin and Matsumoto-Gromyko;

(3) the only remaining problem was the territorial one; and

(4) a peace treaty naturally included territorial settlement and the absence of the clause made no substantive difference.

The Soviet interpretation is that the very stipulation regarding the transfer of Habomai and Shikotan and the deletion of the clause concerning the territorial problem reflected Japan's choice and the settlement of her territorial claim. The exchange of the Matsumoto-Gromyko notes occurred prior to the negotiations in Moscow, which, as it turned out, included renegotiations on the territorial problem. This was contrary to the intent of the Matsumoto-Gromyko notes. In fact, Khrushchev reminded Kono that the Soviet Union had understood that Japan would not touch on the territorial problem when Kono requested prompt return of Habomai and Shikotan on October 16. The Soviet Union was apprised of the Japanese government's position on October 13, 1956, only after Hatoyama and his entourage arrived in Moscow (Matsumoto, 1966: 144-145).[6]

The Soviet Union need not deny the validity of the Matsumoto-Gromyko notes, nor for that matter the Japanese assertion that the territorial problem remains open to discussion. For the territorial problem, the Soviets could argue, does not refer to the Japanese claim to the so-called Northern Territories, but refers to the question of Japan's formal, explicit confirmation of Soviet sovereignty over southern Sakhalin and the Kuriles. Regarding the Joint Declaration, the Soviet government is on record as rejecting the Japanese claim that the Soviet Union agreed to continue negotiations over Japan's claim to Northern Territories. In any event the Soviet Union does not maintain that the Joint Declaration conferred on the U.S.S.R. the titles or rights to these territories. The Soviet Union would welcome Japan's explicit acknowledgement, in the form of a peace treaty, of Soviet sovereignty over these islands. The territorial problem may be said to depend upon this factor.

The American Position

In response to a Soviet memorandum of November 20, 1950, the U.S. government indicated on December 28 that the Yalta Agreement was subject to confirmation by a peace treaty to be concluded in consultation with the powers that participated in the war against Japan (Murthy, 1964: 274). In April 1951, Dulles (1951: 577) stated that the Yalta Agreement was simply "a statement of common purpose by the heads of the three participating powers and not, in itself, an instrument of legal effects". At the San Francisco Conference, which began on September 5, 1951, Dulles, in referring to Part 2(c) of the draft treaty, said that the Allies were to observe only the Potsdam surrender terms and that they were not bound by private understandings among certain Allied governments. Dulles clarified that the Habomai Islands were not included in the geographic term "Kurile Islands" and suggested that any dispute in this matter be referred to the International Court of Justice (Murthy, 1964: 274).

In response to an inquiry by the Japanese government, the U.S. government expressed the following views in early July 1955 (Hoppo Ryodo Fukki Kisei Domei, 1967: 42-43):

1. The Habomais and Shikotan are an integral part of Hok-

kaido, geographically, historically, and legally, and not part of the Kuriles.

2. The Yalta Agreement is a statement of common purpose by the leaders of the participating powers and is not in itself a legally effective instrument. Since the Potsdam Proclamation does not mention the Yalta Agreement, the provisions of the Agreement are not binding on Japan. The conclusion of the Yalta Agreement predates the Potsdam Proclamation and hence cannot determine or interpret Paragraph 8 of that Proclamation (in response to the question whether Paragraph 8 of the Potsdam Proclamation refers to the Yalta Agreement).

3. The Potsdam Proclamation stipulates that the final determination of the Japanese territory will be made later by the participating countries. The Soviet Union cannot solely and unilaterally declare southern Sakhalin or the Kuriles to be its own territories under Paragraph 8 of the Potsdam Proclamation.

4. None of the following three has determined the final status of the territories: General Order Number 1 of the SCAP, the Decree # 677 of the Headquarters of Allied Forces, or Article 2 of the San Francisco Treaty.

5. The final disposition of southern Sakhalin and the Kuriles has not been made and is a matter to be determined by international agreement.

In October 1955, Japan made another official inquiry to the U.S. government concerning Etorofu and Kunashiri. The U.S. response was that (Hoppo Ryodo Fukki Kisei Domei, 1967: 42-43):

1. At Yalta there was no geographic definition of the Kuriles, nor was there a discussion of the history of the Kuriles. The Yalta Agreement was not intended to transfer territories, nor has it any legal effect. There is no record that the parties to the Yalta Conference had intended to allow the Soviet Union to acquire any territory that had not been former Russian territory. The definition of the Kuriles is not given in the peace treaty nor in the minutes of the San Francisco Conference. The U.S. view is that any dispute regarding the Kuriles should be settled by submitting it to the International Court of Justice, according to Article 22.

2. Future international rulings will determine the ultimate

disposition of southern Sakhalin and the Kuriles. The United States has no objection to Japan's attempt to persuade the Soviet Union to return those two islands on the grounds that they do not constitute part of the Kuriles. If unsuccessful, Japan may demand that the Soviet Union agree to submit the question of the extent of the Kuriles to the International Court of Justice. Alternatively, on the grounds that Etorofu and Kunashiri are not part of the Kuriles, Japan may reach some kind of agreement with the Soviet Union concerning these islands in return for stipulating in a Soviet-Japanese peace treaty Japan's renunciation of claims to southern Sakhalin and the Kuriles.

At the request of Foreign Minister Shigemitsu, the U.S. government (Department of State Bulletin, 1956: 484) sent a memorandum of September 7, 1956, which reads in part:

> After careful examination of the historical facts, the United States has reached the conclusion that the islands of Etorofu and Kunashiri (along with the Habomais and Shikotan) have always been a part of Japan proper and should, in justice, be acknowledged as under Japanese sovereignty.

The Soviet Position

The Soviet claim to the Kuriles (including Etorofu and Kunashiri) is based primarily on legal argument, but history is also cited. According to articles in the journals *Sovietsky Float* and *Problems of History*, and the official government newspaper, *Izvestia,* the contention is made that Russian explorers landed on the Kuriles and conquered them prior to the Japanese, and that the residents of the Kuriles were first of Russian nationality (Hoppo Ryodo Fukki Kisei Domei, 1967: 15-19). To cite one of the most recent articles, the November 13, 1970, issue of *Izvestia* (1970a) contains the following passages:

> The Japanese revanchists' arguments that the Kurile Islands are "age-old Japanese territory" seem clumsy and false. Russian explorers got to know the Kuriles as early as 1632, when no one on those islands even knew that such a country as Japan existed. When

> discovered by the Russians, the Kuriles and Sakhalin were inhabited by the Ainus, and also by Siberian nationalities. . . . Even much later, in 1726, Russian navigators did not see a single Japanese on the Kuriles. There could not have been any Japanese there, since the laws of that time, under the rule of the Tokugawa Shoguns, forbade the Japanese to leave their country or to build ships for long voyages on pain of death. . . . The Japanese historians . . . wrote that not only Sakhalin and the Kurile Islands but even the island of Yezo (now Hokkaido) were not regarded as possessions of Japan until the middle of the 19th century.

Japan disputes the historical facts cited in Russian publications and argues that the important issue is not who discovered the Kuriles first but rather who effectively *ruled* the areas.

The basic position of the Soviet Union is that the territorial question has already been resolved by a series of international agreements. The stipulation in the Yalta Agreement is unequivocal: it states explicitly that southern Sakhalin be returned and that the Kuriles be handed over to the Soviet Union. According to the Soviet view, the Potsdam Proclamation stipulates that the provisions of the Cairo Declaration be carried out and that Paragraph 8 of the proclamation is actually based on the Yalta Agreement. Their central argument is that the Yalta Agreement and the Potsdam Proclamation are indivisible. The Soviets reject the Japanese assertion that a determination for "the minor islands" mentioned in the proclamation has not been made.

As Khrushchev (1966) wrote to Ikeda, the Potsdam Proclamation restricts Japanese sovereignty to the four main islands and a few small islands. By signing the Instrument of Surrender, Japan pledged faithful implementation of the provisions of the Potsdam Proclamation. *Since the Kuriles are excluded from the territories left under Japanese sovereignty, Japan's present claim violates the above pledge.*

According to the Soviet view, the Japanese contention that the Yalta Agreement is not binding on her because of nonparticipation is an absurdity, having no basis in international law. Although Japan was not a signatory, "by having capitulated, it accepted all provisions laid down in Yalta by the Allied powers, who proceeded from the existing agreements between them, including the Yalta Agreement" (Quoted in Hayes, 1972: 24).

Khrushchev asserted that since the Yalta Agreement was concluded among powers fighting against Japan, Japan naturally was not, nor could have been, a signatory. Moreover, Japan, by its surrender, accepted the conditions upon which the Allied powers had agreed. With regard to this point, the Allied powers used the agreements existing among them as a basis for the Yalta Agreement (Khrushchev, 1966: 235-236).

Another major Soviet argument in the Kuriles dispute is that the San Francisco Peace Treaty has conclusively and irrevocably settled the territorial problem; that Japan renounced all rights, titles, and claims to southern Sakhalin and the Kuriles. Even though the Soviet Union is not a signatory, Japan's renunciation under Article 2 is legally binding *on Japan.* Japan's obligation under the peace treaty is based on wartime agreements among the Allied powers and the Instrument of Surrender. Japan's claim, therefore, constitutes an attempt to revise the results of World War II and of the conditions of the peace treaty (Khrushchev, 1966: 235-236).

According to the Soviet view, no distinction was ever made among the Kuriles at Yalta, in General Order Number 1, nor in the San Francisco Treaty. Both refer to the *entire* Kuriles chain. No basis exists for the contention that Etorofu and Kunashiri were not included. Numerous Japanese publications from prewar days attest to this position, and the Japanese government acknowledged more than once in the postwar period that these islands were part of the Kuriles (Khrushchev, 1966: 235-236).

The Soviets consider Etorofu and Kunashiri to be integral parts of the Kuriles. There is no basis for Japan's assertion that the two are not included in the term "Kuriles" as it is used in the peace treaty. If Japan's sovereignty extends to these two islands, the Soviets ask, why did Japan sign the peace treaty, or why did she not at least enter a reservation? (Sugiwara, 1965: 144).

Japan's claim on the basis of the Treaties of Shimada and St. Petersburg is rejected by the Soviet Union. They reason that Japan initiated a war of aggression against Russia in 1904 and by doing so Japan violated those treaties, relinquishing the right to invoke their provisions. Moreover, Japan invaded northern Sakhalin and Siberia in the 1920s, by that action violating the

Treaty of 1905 (Sugiwara, 1965: 141; Nampo Doho Engo Kai, 1966: 236). Despite this, the Soviet view holds, the Soviet Union made a substantial concession in 1956 by offering to transfer Habomai and Shikotan at such time as a peace treaty was concluded.

Escalation of the Territorial Dispute: 1960-1972

It will be recalled that in 1956 the Soviet Union made a commitment to transfer the Habomais and Shikotan to Japan after a peace treaty was concluded. However, this offer may not be viable today, since the Soviet Union added a stipulation on January 27, 1960, that the islands would be returned only on the condition that all foreign troops be withdrawn from Japan and that a peace treaty be signed between the two countries. Since this stipulation has not been officially withdrawn, presumably it is still operative. When it was made, the Soviet Union was objecting to the conclusion of the revised U.S.-Japan Security Treaty (January 19, 1960). It contended that the treaty deprived Japan of its independence from the American occupation forces remaining in Japan, rendering it impossible for the Soviet Union to fulfill its promise. It viewed the treaty as directed against the Soviet Union as well as against the People's Republic of China, and took the position that it could not contribute to the extension of territory available to foreign troops by turning the islands over to Japan (Nampo Doho Engo Kai, 1966: 188-191).

In a note of rebuttal to the Soviets on February 6, 1960, Japan stated that it could not recognize the Soviet Union's unilateral attempt to add new conditions and change the contents of the Joint Declaration of 1956. The Soviet response, in its note of February 25, 1960, asserted that the Security Treaty with the United States contradicted the Joint Declaration of 1956 and violated Japan's obligation to develop good-neighbor relations with the Soviet Union. It further asserted that Japan's demand for the return of territories other than Habomai and Shikotan was a manifestation of a dangerous trend toward revanchism. It also accused Japan of deliberately delaying the conclusion of a peace treaty by presenting unfounded territorial demands that had previously been settled by various international agreements (Nampo Doho Engo Kai, 1966: 194-196). The Japanese rebuttal note of March 1, 1960, stated that the territorial problem had not been settled and must await a peace treaty, which the Soviet Union had promised to discuss in 1956. It added that it was only natural for Japan to "seek transfer of Etorofu and Kunashiri which are inherent Japanese territory", and expressed total consternation at the Soviet Union's characterization of the heartfelt wishes of all Japanese for the return of these inherent territories as revanchism (Nampo Doho Engo Kai, 1966: 197-199).

The Soviet reply of April 22, 1960, is informative since it presented the Soviet interpretation of the Joint Declaration. Phrasing the problem as an "unfounded claim to Soviet territory", the note stated that the government of Japan "asserts arbitrarily as though both sides had agreed by the Joint Declaration to regard the territorial problem as having been left to future deliberation. In actuality there was no such agreement and such an agreement could not have been made and that the Soviet government rejects the Japanese assertion. The territorial problem between the U.S.S.R. and Japan has been determined by International agreements concerned" (Nampo Doho Engo Kai, 1966: 199-211).

On Mikoyan's visit to Japan in August 1961, Khrushchev sent a personal letter to Prime Minister Ikeda, expressing his desire for "complete normalization" of relations between the two countries "by adjusting all of the unsettled questions". Ikeda responded on August 26, 1961, that the conclusion of a peace treaty was necessary for complete normalization, and that it was the Soviet government that could open the road to a peace treaty by returning inherent Japanese territories. In his note of September 29, 1961, Khrushchev stated that the territorial problem had long been settled by a series of international agreements and that the Japanese government was trying to create artificial barriers in the path to full normalization by raising this problem. "How could the problem of reversion to Japan by non-Japanese territory be raised?" retorted Khrushchev. He added that by raising this question, Japan was also trying to avoid recognizing the relevant stipulation of the San Francisco Treaty and that such an attitude could only cause deterioration in Soviet-Japanese relations (Nampo Doho Engo Kai, 1966: 223-233).

Following Ikeda's reply of November 15, 1961, containing a

refutation of the Soviet contention that the problem had been resolved, Khrushchev sent another memorandum on December 8, 1961. This memorandum contained a fairly lengthy Soviet argument on the northern territorial issue and represented a most authoritative Soviet exposition of its position on the issue. Major points made were similar to those described above in the section on the Soviet position (Nampo Doho Engo Kai, 1966: 233-236).

On January 4, 1964, Khrushchev made a proposal for the non-use of force in the settlement of territorial disputes and the problem of national boundaries. In his response of February 7, 1964, Ikeda referred to "the most important unresolved issue of the Northern Territories", expressing his desire for a fair and speedy resolution of the territorial problem (Nampo Doho Engo Kai, 1966: 241-242).

During the visit of a group of Supreme Soviet deputies, led by Mikoyan in May 1964, Khrushchev sent another personal message to Ikeda repeating his desire for the conclusion of a peace treaty so as to fully and finally normalize the relations between the two countries. In response, on May 26, 1964, Ikeda reiterated his view that a peace treaty was essential to provide a permanent basis for the establishment of good-neighbor relations and that Japan was prepared to conclude such a peace treaty if the return of "our inherent territories" was realized (Nampo Doho Engo Kai, 1966: 242-243). At the press conference given at the end of his stay in Tokyo, Mikoyan was asked about the northern territorial issue. He replied that the Soviet Union stood by the San Francisco Treaty and the 1956 Joint Declaration. When asked specifically, he rejected the Japanese view that Etorofu and Kunashiri were traditionally Japanese (New Times, 1964: 4-8).

In the course of the visit of the Japanese parliamentary delegation to the Soviet Union in September 1964, Ikeda dispatched a personal letter to Khrushchev calling for a speedy return of Japan's inherent territories, followed by the conclusion of a peace treaty. It was at a meeting with the visiting Japanese parliamentarians that Khrushchev remarked that the Habomais and Shikotan would be returned if the United States returned Okinawa to Japan:

I remember the agreement that we reached with your renowned leader, the late Mr. Hatoyama . . . on the specific question of the two islands of Habomai and Shikotan. We still adhere to the agreement. But we declared that we would give these islands to Japan only after we had signed a peace treaty with you. However, so far there is still no peace treaty. Besides, the U.S.A. has its military bases in Japan, it seized Okinawa from you, and it regards Okinawa and Japan itself as a strategic base in its struggle against the Soviet Union and China. If we gave you Habomai and Shikotan in such a situation, your fishermen would be pleased. . . . But the American imperialists . . . have the opportunity to build on your islands military bases aimed against the Soviet Union. We do not want to strengthen American imperialism through our concessions to Japan. If the Americans now left Japan and liberated Okinawa, and if a peace treaty were signed, we would immediately send you a telegram: "Please come and take Habomai and Shikotan in accordance with our agreement" [Pravda, 1964a; Current Digest of Soviet Press, 1964].

Foreign Minister Shiina visited the Soviet Union in January 1966 and attempted to discuss the northern territorial issue, but Soviet leaders refused, saying the problem had been settled. Shiina tried in vain to include a reference to the problem in the communiqué, and returned home, convinced that the Soviet Union's position had not changed at all since its expression in the Joint Declaration. When Gromyko paid a return visit to Japan seven months later, the Soviet aide refused to include a reference to the territorial issue in the communiqué, which noted simply that both sides acknowledged the need for the conclusion of a peace treaty. In fact Gromyko avoided a discussion of the problem on the grounds that a reiteration of the Soviet position, which remained unchanged, would not contribute to the development of Japanese-Soviet relations (Hirano, 1972: 44-45; Hoppo Ryodo Fukki Kisei Domei, 1967: 92).

During Foreign Minister Miki's visit to Moscow the following year, Kosygin introduced the possibility that an *interim document* might be explored through diplomatic channels since neither side apparently knew how to approach the problem of a peace treaty. The news of Kosygin's suggestion aroused much interest in Japan and the expectation of a possible change in the

Soviet position. However, in subsequent talks with Japanese political leaders and officials, the Soviets let it be known that no
change in their position had occurred, i.e., the territorial problem
had been settled, insofar as they were concerned (Hirano, 1972:
46).

In September 1969, during his Moscow meeting with Foreign
Minister Aichi, Kosygin reportedly said that Soviet policy called
for maintaining the territorial status quo determined at the end of
World War II and that the issue of the Northern Territories could
not be considered in relation to Japan alone because any change
would have wider ramifications (Hirano, 1972: 47-48). The impression was thereby created that the Soviet rationale for its
position might have changed somewhat, but that the actual position itself, as expressed in publications during that period and
afterward, showed no change whatever.

Soviet criticism of Japan's alleged militarism and revanchism
grew in intensity following Prime Minister Sato's reference to the
Northern Territories in his speech at the 25th commemoration
session of the U.N. General Assembly in October 1970. Sato
blamed the inability of the two sides to conclude a peace treaty
on the lack of progress in talks with the Soviet Union over
territories which he said were "inherent to Japan".

Soviet displeasure was evident. A week after Sato's speech,
Izvestia (1970c) denounced the Japanese campaign for the return
of the Northern Territories, maintaining that, contrary to the
impression left by Sato, no talks on the question were in progress.
Said *Izvestia*:

> In any case this is academic (the question was conclusively and
> irrevocably resolved long ago) . . . Sato's address actually has the
> ring of an appeal for reconsideration of the results of the Second
> World War. Regardless of what Japanese politicians may call it in
> their speeches, that is also revanchism. The Prime Minister's discus-
> sion of the "northern territories" was essentially an appeal for
> revision of the 1951 San Francisco Treaty, under which Japan
> officially abandoned all claim to the Kuriles Inslands. . . . But the
> Soviet Union and the Soviet public cannot dismiss statements and
> pronouncements that deal with the question of Soviet territorial
> integrity and call for revision of the results of the Second World
> War.

Another attack was published in its November 13, 1970 issue. This time *Izvestia* (1970b) stressed the following points:

(1) everything connected with the revanchist campaign was blessed by Japanese authorities, including the observance of a "month dedicated to the return of the Northern Territories" featuring rallies and demonstrations participated in by officials;

(2) revanchist aspirations were now part of Japan's diplomatic activity, and the Ministry of Foreign Affairs had distributed official materials, distorting history by claiming that the Kuriles were "age-old Japanese territory";

(3) irresponsible demonstrations by revanchists were taking place outside the Soviet Embassy in Tokyo and the Consulate General in Sapporo;

(4) the revanchist campaign at least in part reflected the desire of the ruling circles to bring Japan's "armed forces into correspondence with its growing economic possibilities", and the "artificial" emphasis on the Northern Territories problem was designed to further the interests of the circles inside Japan and elsewhere opposed to the development of good-neighbor relations with the Soviet Union and to the strengthening of peace in Asia and the Far East;

(5) attempts to revise the borders were contrary to tendencies in present-day international relations, as had been demonstrated by the recently concluded treaty between the Soviet Union and the Federal Republic of Germany.

In addition, Soviet Chargé d'Affaires A.P. Okonishnikov delivered a verbal protest to the Japanese government accusing Japanese officials of artificially magnifying the reversion movement, and protesting as "unfriendly" the following actions taken by Japan:

(1) establishment of the Okinawa-Northern Territories Agency;

(2) inspections of the northern areas by Diet members;

(3) distribution at the U.N. of documents on the northern territorial issue;

(4) demonstrations outside the Soviet Embassy in Tokyo; and

(5) Prime Minister Sato's reference to the issue before the U.N. General Assembly in October 1970 (Japan Report, 1970: 4).

Japan's reply came in the form of a counter-protest by Foreign Vice-Minister Haruki Mori to Okonishnikov on November 17. Mori told the Soviet diplomat that since the Japanese government and the National Diet had been attacked for their domestic actions, the Soviet Union was interfering in the internal affairs of Japan. He argued that with the reversion of Okinawa settled, it was only natural for attention to focus on the Northern Territories, and insisted that the movement was entirely spontaneous, denying the Soviet charge of revanchism. He blamed the problem on the Soviet's illegal occupation of "inherent" Japanese territory, calling it "inconsistent with international justice for the Soviet Government to willfully impose its unilateral measure on another country without any legal basis". Emphasizing that the conclusion of a peace treaty, through prompt return of the four islands, would contribute not only to the betterment of relations with the Soviet Union, but to the promotion of peace and security in Asia as well, Mori expressed the expectation of the Japanese government that the Soviet Union would take prompt and positive action (Japan Report, 1970: 4-5).

This time the Soviet reply, another ringing denunciation of Japanese "revanchists", was printed in *Pravda* (1970), the organ of the Communist Party. It said, in part:

> But Japanese officials believe that reference to the excesses of the revanchist forces are "an attempt to interfere in the internal affairs" of Japan. As for laying claim to other people's land and fomenting hatred against the country's neighbors, that is only a series of internal measures and is "normal". . . . It is the Japanese side that has frustrated the conclusion of a peace treaty between our countries for many years, attempting to replace negotiations on a peace treaty by discussion of the "territorial question", which was resolved long ago. The Japanese government does not conceal the fact that it wants not a real peace treaty but a "peace treaty based on the return of the northern territories", i.e., a revision of the results of the Second World War.

In summary, since 1956 the northern territorial issue has remained the single most important impediment to the conclusion of a peace treaty. Despite Soviet urging, Japan has insisted on the return of the Northern Territories as a precondition, stepping up its own efforts to reopen the issue in bilateral discussions. The Japanese have become increasingly bolder, more vociferous, and more adamant. Seventeen years following the Joint Declaration that restored diplomatic relations between the two countries, Prime Minister Tanaka finally had an opportunity to raise the issue directly at formal summit meetings with Soviet leaders in October 1973.

However, there has been no visible change in the basic Soviet position, i.e., that the territorial problem has long been settled by international agreement. The only shift in recent years is the caution shown by Soviet officials in dismissing outright Japan's claim on that basis. Other rationales, more acceptable or at least less offensive to the Japanese, have been invoked to explain the Soviet Union's negative attitude, and there have been visible signs of cordiality and flexibility. Nevertheless, the basic position has remained the same.

The Summit Meeting of 1973

In the months following the first "Nixon shock", the Japanese detected signs of Soviet flexibility on the issue. The Japanese thought it significant that Gromyko, during his visit to Japan in January 1972, refrained from using the familiar expression, "the matter has been settled". The Japanese ascribed this to a desire to woo Japan away from the United States and prevent a Japanese-Chinese rapprochement. An agreement was made at that time for the two nations to begin negotiations on a peace treaty before the end of 1972. Japan interpreted this to mean negotiations regarding the territorial question.

Prime Minister Tanaka paid an official visit to the Soviet Union from October 7 through October 10, 1973, and discussed the northern territorial issue, among other items, with Soviet leaders. The joint Japanese-Soviet statement issued on October 10 at the conclusion of the talks deserves close attention for what it contains as well as for what it omits. There is *no* direct reference to the territorial problem in the communiqué; however, the Japanese are firm in their understanding that the territorial problem will be included in future negotiations on a peace treaty. The key sentences in the communiqué are that "settlement of outstanding questions, left over since the time of the second world war and the signing of a peace treaty, will make a contribution. . . . The two sides agreed to continue the talks on signing a peace treaty between both countries at an appropriate period in 1974".

These sentences clearly indicate to the Japanese a Soviet agreement to hold talks on the territorial issue, since, in their opinion, the "outstanding questions" refers specifically to the territorial issue. It should be noted that the joint statement mentions outstanding questions (plural, not singular). I have been told privately that the Japanese original draft was in fact in the singular but was changed at the request of the Soviet Union and with explicit Soviet assurance that the unsettled questions included the territorial issue. Moreover, as the Japanese argument goes, the single impediment to the peace treaty between the two countries has been precisely this territorial issue. The most conservative and skeptical interpretation would probably indicate that the territorial issue is at least included among the unsettled questions. The Japanese claim that for the first time the top Soviet leaders conceded that the territorial issue exists, and that Japan successfully placed the matter on the agenda for future negotiation.

Soviet officials, on the other hand, insist in both public and private that there has been no change in their position on the territorial issue. The Soviets believe the Japanese interpretation was advanced as domestic political propaganda and is not warranted. As far as the Soviets are concerned, unsettled questions do *not* include the territorial question but refer rather to such questions as "safe fishing". Thus, the Soviets dismiss the Japanese interpretation as unfounded and self-serving.

There are a number of discrepancies between the Russian and the Japanese texts of the communiqué. One that caused much commotion in Japan was the omission in the Russian version of any reference to continued discussion of the problem of safe fishing. After an exchange of notes, the Soviet government finally acknowledged the accuracy of the Japanese text. A comparison of the Japanese and Russian versions reveals subtle differences in meaning concerning paragraph one of the communiqué. The sense of the Japanese version is the signing of a peace treaty is to be preceded by a settlement of those outstanding questions that would make a contribution to friendly relations between the two countries. In the Russian version, both the settlement of outstanding questions *and* the signing of a peace treaty will make such a contribution. In other words, in the Russian version, the conclusion of a peace treaty does *not* presuppose the settlement of outstanding questions, while the Japanese version reads as though the signing of a peace treaty is to follow, not to antecede, the settlement of such questions.

The remarks made by Tanaka and Ohira at press conferences on October 10 and 11, 1973, are very suggestive in this regard. Tanaka was asked if it had been confirmed that the clause concerning "outstanding questions" included the territorial problem. He responded, "there are no such things as outstanding problems which do not include the territorial problem". "Of course", he added, "such problems as safe fishing are also included". When pressed as to whether the Soviet Union had the same understanding that the status of Etorofu and Kunashiri was to be included in the clause, he asked the reporters to take into account the statement he had made the previous day, to the effect that *Pravda* carried the entire text of his luncheon speech containing his reference to the northern territorial issue (Gaimusho, 1973: 34-35). According to a Japanese newspaper report (Mainichi Shimbun, 1973c) from Moscow, the Japanese desire for inclusion of the phrase "territorial problem" in the communiqué and the Soviet refusal resulted in a compromise, suggested by the Soviet Union, that the entire text of Tanaka's speech be printed in *Pravda* the following morning.

Tanaka stated at these press conferences that the Soviet leaders seemed to understand that the territorial issue constituted the most important unsettled problem. However, he added, the Soviet position was that the problem was complicated and could not be resolved overnight; it would require continued talks in good faith on both sides. Tanaka described his activities in Moscow not as "negotiations", but rather as a candid exchange of views and informal exploratory talks between himself and Brezhnev (Gaimusho, 1973: 28, 35).

Nikkaido, Chief Cabinet Secretary, stated unequivocally that "unsettled questions" referred to the Northern Territories (Mainichi Shimbun, 1973b). Both Tanaka and Ohira remained silent as to the specific position the Soviet Union took on the substance of the territorial issue. Tanaka's own account was that in response to Japan's request for the return of the Northern Territories, the Soviet side said that "it is only yesterday that you raised formally the territorial problem. It is unreasonable to expect for it to be resolved today. No matter how dictatorial you may be". Tanaka added that he had not quite expected to be called a dictator at the Kremlin. He claimed his accomplishment was that he finally "placed the question on the table" (Gaimusho, 1973: 35).

In the words of Ohira, Japan "has succeeded in bringing the matter into the arena for concrete negotiation", or Japan "has laid a track for negotiation". When asked whether he obtained confirmation from the Russian side that the outstanding questions clause referred to the territorial problem (more specifically, as it included Etorofu and Kunashiri), Ohira was evasive. He responded by describing the Soviet position that, other than the territorial problem, there are such matters as the basic principles of economic cooperation, mutual renunciation of force, and various fundamental elements affecting the relations between governments that should be included in a peace treaty, and hence the "unsettled problem" is not a singular one. When asked if there was any change in the substance of the Soviet position on the territorial issue, Ohira was again evasive. This time, he responded that the Soviet Union consistently avoided the expression "territory" in the communiqué. When asked whether Etorofu and Kunashiri would be included in the next year's negotiations, Ohira answered, "Of course. We have no intention to divide up the territories in proceeding to negotiation" (Gaimusho, 1973: 30-32). Thus, Japan's intention and determination persistently to carry on negotiations on the territorial matter is crystal clear. However, both Tanaka and Ohira have remained evasive on the exact terms of the Soviet position regarding both the substance of the territorial issue and the question of whether that issue was included in the outstanding questions clause.

Whether the summit diplomacy constituted a major step forward for Japan remains to be seen. The Soviet Union agreed in private and informally that the territorial problem would be discussed, i.e., that "outstanding questions" included the territorial problem. This may represent some progress from Japan's point of view, but it does not mean that the Soviet Union's substantive position has changed. This writer was impressed with the tenacity and intensity with which the Soviet officials insisted in private that the term "outstanding questions" does *not* include the territorial problem.

A Japanese reporter interviewed Mr. Kudryavtsev of *Izvestia* two days after the end of the summit conference. Kudryavtsev was pleased with the result of the conference, especially with the agreement to promote economic cooperation between the two countries. When the reporter said that the communiqué contained a clause about the outstanding problems, Kudryavtsev stated that that did not represent a change in Soviet position. When asked again whether the Soviet attitude represented a change, he replied that there was no word about the territorial problem in the official documents. He went on to say that to promote or incite this problem would impede Japanese-Soviet negotiations and put the brakes on the development of Japanese-Soviet relations. He thought the need for oil for Japan much more important than two or four islands. He added, "why don't we look at larger problems instead of only thinking of the territorial problem". He explained that when Ishida, a Japanese parliamentarian, visited him earlier he was told that resolution of the northern territorial problem was the earnest wish of the entire Japanese nation, whereupon he told Ishida that the Soviet Union also had to deal with public opinion, which opposed the return of the islands (Mainichi Shimbun, 1973a).

Ovchinikov of *Pravda*, responding to the question by an *Asahi* reporter on the eve of the closing of the summit conference, reiterated that the Japanese position is not conducive to the promotion of Soviet-Japanese relations. He felt that the forces in Japan that do not desire improved relations were appealing to nationalism, trying to destroy friendly understanding between the two countries. He thought that both sides should begin by agreeing on whatever is mutually acceptable. No forward movement would be made under the logic that a solution of one problem presupposes the solution of another. He stated that the official position of the Soviet government on the northern territorial issue would be the same as it was in 1960 (Asahi Shimbun, 1973b).

Motivations Underlying the Soviet Position

Several major considerations appear to underlie Soviet refusal to relinquish these islands. First, the Soviets fear that the return of the disputed territory would not wholly satisfy the Japanese; that they would then demand the northern part of the Kuriles and, eventually, southern Sakhalin as well. This Soviet suspicion is indicated in Kudryavtsev's article in *Izvestia* on November 13, 1970, where he refers to the revanchists' "step-by-step demands". There is some ground for Soviet suspicion. Some opposition parties have laid claim to a greater area of the Kuriles than has the ruling party. This aspect will be examined later. In view of the Japanese position on the final disposition of the Northern Territories, if the Soviet Union returns Etorofu and Kunashiri it might weaken the Soviet legal claim to the northern Kuriles and southern Sakhalin as well.

Secondly, Soviet concessions on this matter would open up a Pandora's box—other countries with territorial grievances against the Soviet Union would be encouraged to pursue them. It should be remembered that the People's Republic of China supports Japan's claim to the Northern Territories, which surely enhanced Soviet sensitivity to the territorial issue; hence their insistence that the post-World War II boundaries remain final (Pravda, 1964b; International Affairs, 1964: 80; Izvestia, 1972).

Chinese support for Japan's position is well known.[7] To take a few recent examples, Chou En-lai told a Japanese visitor, Kimura Takeo, on January 10, 1973, that Mao's statement of 1964 affirming Japan's right to recover the entire Kuriles island chain remains the Chinese position today. A political report of the 19th Party Congress contains a passage to the effect that if the Soviet Union is interested in the movement toward international détente, why doesn't it demonstrate its sincerity by returning the four islands to the Japanese?

In his talks with the visiting Japanese parliamentarians on September 15, 1964, Khrushchev touched on Chinese claims to Soviet territory. Afterward, *Pravda* carried a lengthy denunciation of the Chinese for Mao's support of the Japanese claim, and for their own claims as well:

Indeed by betraying the interests of peace, the revolution and Socialism, Mao Tse-tung and his supporters have practically joined hands with the ultra-reactionary circles of the Japanese monopoly bourgeoisie. In his double-dyed anti-Sovietism, Mao went so far as to support the Japanese revanchists' claims to a part of Soviet territory—the Kurile Islands—during a talk with a delegation of Japanese Socialists in the summer of 1964.

Mao Tse-tung's main preoccupation is with whipping up anti-Soviet sentiment, and playing on the nationalistic feelings of the most reactionary forces . . .

He is not just claiming Soviet territory but presenting his claims as part of a "general territorial question . . . "

Chinese spokesmen have lately been referring more and more frequently to hundreds of thousands of square kilometers of Soviet territory as allegedly belonging "by right" to China . . .

Now, in his talk, Mao Tse-tung declares: "About 100 years ago the area to the east of Baikal became the territory of Russia, and since then Vladivostok, Khabarovsk, Kamchatka and other points have been the territory of the Soviet Union. We have not yet presented a bill on this account".

By what right do the Chinese leaders lay claim to areas which did not belong to China? . . .

What would happen if all states were to follow the Peking recipe and started presenting each other with claims for the revision of historically evolved frontiers?

The rulers of the capitalist world have for some time been keeping an eye on the Chinese leaders' nationalism and great-Power proclivities. It was, therefore, no accident that the Japanese Right-wing Socialists also came up with a question about the Kuriles and put it to Mao Tse-tung and the C.P.C. Chairman gave them the answer they wanted [International Affairs, 1964: 80-84].

The February 4, 1972 issue of *Izvestia* states that the reason the Chinese are supporting Japan's claims to the Northern Territories is to realize their own world strategy of anti-Sovietism and their own hegemonic aspirations. It argues that Peking's support is provocative and designed to stir up revanchist and nationalistic passions in certain circles in Japan.

Thirdly, the Soviets feel that time is on their side. The longer the status quo continues, with the Soviets in control, the greater the validity of the Soviet claims to the islands. Remembering what occurred with the two Germanys, and Soviet relations with them, they believe a day will come when Japan will be resigned to her present boundaries. This sentiment was expressed to me by several Soviet scholars. Soviet preference for a German solution is evident in the following passage:

> This position on the part of the Japanese ruling circles is close to the bankrupt position of former West German governments, which made revanchism, border revision and claims to other people's land their official policy. This policy led to complications in the situation in Europe and was doomed to failure by the course of history. The conclusion of treaties between the U.S.S.R. and the F.R.G. and between Poland and the F.R.G. affirming the inviolability of the postwar borders in Europe reflects a new trend in the development of the international situation, one that corresponds to interests of peace and security [Pravda, 1970; Current Digest of Soviet Press, 1970].

Fourthly, the Soviet military is reportedly opposed to the return of the disputed territory because of its strategic value. According to the Soviet Navy the Kuriles (including Etorofu and Kunashiri) constitute a protective shield for the Soviet Far East and provide the Navy with relative security and a convenient access for operations in the Pacific. During the negotiations leading to the Treaty of St. Petersburg, the Russians were opposed to Japan gaining the entire Kuriles on the grounds that the Russian fleet could not pass the Strait (presumably Shumshu Strait). They proposed that Japan obtain the Kuriles south of Onekotan in return for giving up Sakhalin (Hoppo Ryodo Fukki Kisei Domei, 1967: 13-14; Mainichi Shimbun, 1973).

On May 26, 1964, Mikoyan told Premier Ikeda that Etorofu and Kunashiri were small islands but important as a gateway to Kamchatka, and could not be abandoned. On July 14, 1964, Khrushchev told a group of Japanese socialists that Etorofu and Kunashiri had no economic value but were militarily important, for essentially the same reasons: they are a gateway to Kamchatka and constitute a Soviet defense line. He repeated the same view to a group of Japanese visitors on September 15, 1964; evidently referring to Habomai and Shikotan, Khrushchev stated them to be of small economic value but of great strategic and defense importance to the Soviet Union (Hoppo Ryodo Fukki Kisei Domei, 1967: 14).

Motivations Underlying the Japanese Claim

The Japanese are under no illusions, it should be pointed out, that the Soviets will return the islands. They concede the Soviet fear of adverse repercussions on other territorial claims and, more fundamentally, are convinced that the U.S.S.R. simply cannot be expected to relinquish any territory it has already acquired. The question is, then, why do the Japanese continue to raise the issue when they themselves entertain no realistic expectation of a return of the islands? Several considerations are operating here.

The question of territory evokes nationalistic sentiments that no politician, including those on the left, can afford to ignore. With the single exception of the ruling conservative party (the LDP), all other political parties have laid claim to the *entire* Kuriles, though the wordings of their respective formal positions vary somewhat, reflecting perhaps differing degrees of conviction.

The *Komeito* and the Democratic Socialist Party (DSP) share the view of the LDP that the return of the Northern Territories (four islands) should be a precondition for the conclusion of a peace treaty, but go further than the LDP in asserting that Japan should negotiate with the Soviet Union with regard to the northern Kuriles *following* the conclusion of such a treaty (Sugiyama, 1972: 34-36; Komei Shimbun, 1973).

The Japanese Communist Party (JCP) and Japan Socialist Party (JSP) urge speedy conclusion of a peace treaty. The JSP also calls for immediate return of Habomai and Shikotan, and urges that, upon the dissolution of the U.S.-Japan Security Treaty, continued efforts be made to realize restoration of the entire Kuriles, northern and southern, to Japan (Nihon Shakaito Senkyo Taisaku Iinkai, 1972: 32).

Reconfirming the Japan-Soviet Joint Declaration, the JCP calls for immediate conclusion of a peace treaty, development of friendly relations between the two countries on the basis of five principles of peace, and an attempt to realize the return of Habomai and Shikotan. The JCP is opposed to the positions of the LDP and others, which they say delays the conclusion of a peace treaty on the basis of "sophistry that Kunashiri and Etorofu are not included in the Kuriles." After abrogating the Security Treaty with the United States, the JCP would seek talks with the Soviet Union on the return of the Kuriles. As for Article II(c), the JCP would inform all countries concerned of Japan's abrogation of that portion of the article dealing with the renunciation of the Kuriles (Akahata, 1971).

Though the JCP and JSP come closer to the Soviet position on the urgency of a peace treaty, both parties, to the dismay of the Soviet Union, continue to say that they would "seek to realize the return of the entire Kuriles" following a peace treaty. It should be added here that a peace treaty is generally considered to represent a final territorial settlement; how these two leftwing parties would try to realize the return of the Kuriles *after* the conclusion of a peace treaty is still unclear.

The *Komeito* and the DSP hold identical views that the return of Etorofu and Kunashiri should be a precondition for signing a peace treaty; however, their position goes beyond the LDP in expecting continued negotiations concerning the return of the northern Kuriles later. The LDP remains reticent on the northern Kuriles, but on some occasions states that the Japanese government will be prepared to stipulate in a peace treaty with the Soviet Union the fact of Japan's renunciation—presumably without specifying the beneficiary.

The state of public opinion on the issue is relevant, and a brief review of the results of opinion polls is in order. According to a nationwide survey conducted by *Kyodo* press in November 1969 and November 1972, about 60 percent of the public expressed varying degrees of interest in the northern territorial issue. The *Sankei* newspaper polls conducted in the Tokyo and Osaka areas indicate about 70 percent showing varying degrees of interest.

An unpublished (nationwide) government survey indicates that approximately 40 percent of the public favored the conclusion of a peace treaty on the condition that the four islands be returned to Japan; that about 23 percent favored the conclusion of a peace treaty with the two islands of Habomai and Shikotan returned, leaving the question of the other islands to the future. About 9 percent could not say one way or the other; 28 percent were "unclear" or "didn't know"; 11% "had no opinion". The bulk of those who chose the second option said that Japan should press positively for the return of the rest of the islands after the conclusion of a peace treaty. Fourteen percent thought this could not be avoided if the Soviet Union did not return these islands.

The *Sankei* survey of March 1973 in the Tokyo-Osaka areas used slightly different phrases. About 52 percent of the sample (1000) were in favor of "step-by-step" return", i.e., the return of Habomei and Shikotan first, and then continued negotiations regarding the others. Of the sample, a minority (33 percent) thought that Japan should persist in demanding the return of all four islands because they were "inherent territory".

The *Kyodo* poll of November 1969 and November 1972 (a nationwide sample of 3000) showed the following results:

Question: In negotiating with the Soviet Union, what would you do?

	November 1969	November 1972
1. Realize the return of Habomai and Shikotan and continue negotiations on Kunashiri and Etorofu	19.5%	14.1%
2. Seek the return of all four islands as one whole	11.8%	13.8%
3. Seek the return of the entire Kuriles	26.5%	17.2%
4. Seek the return of southern Sakhalin in addition to the Kuriles	8.4%	15.7%
5. Don't know	33.8%	39.2%

The striking features of these results are that the proportion supporting options 1 and 2 are about equal, and, more surprisingly, about one-third of the public says it would demand the return of the *entire* Kuriles and about half would demand the return of southern Sakhalin as well.

The *Yomiuiri* newspaper conducted a poll of a sample of the "elite public" and university students. The elite sample of 168 consisted of individuals from academia, commentators, leaders of mass media, economic leaders, bureaucrats, members of the SDF, and Defense Agency civilians. The other sample was made up of 366 students at 19 universities, majoring in international politics. The results were published on June 27, 1973:

Question: With what attitude should one approach the northern territorial problem?

	Elite	Students
1. Demand the return of the four islands and not conclude a peace treaty until that is realized	30.4%	12.6%
2. First conclude a peace treaty with the return of Habomai and Shikotan, and then continue negotiations on Etorofu and Kunashiri	34.5%	28.4%
3. Give up the idea of regaining Etorofu and Kunashiri	.6%	.8%
4. Agree to pay economic compensation for the return (no territories are specified)	4.8%	10.4%
5. Not be too concerned with the return (of the islands) if safe fishing is allowed in northern waters	4.2%	16.7%
6. While not abandoning the territories, not make a commotion over the issue	18.5%	10.1%
7. Not be so concerned with the return as to sacrifice friendly relations with the Soviet Union	4.2%	15.0%
8. Abandon the issue, since the Soviet position is correct	0.0%	0.0%
9. Either way is all right (it doesn't matter)	.6%	1.4%

Several observations seem warranted on the basis of the *Yomiuri* survey data:

(1) a step-by-step approach is supported by 34.5 percent of the elite public and 28.4 percent of the student sample;

(2) the position of the Japanese government is supported by 30.4 percent and 12.6 percent of the samples respectively;

(3) those who think Japan should give up Etorofu and Kunashiri altogether are less than 1 percent;

(4) no one takes the position that the Soviet position is correct and that hence Japan should give up the Northern Territories;

(5) overall, the Japanese desire to recover the islands has the widespread support of the elite public. The government's position on a peace treaty has the support of one-third of the sample.

It appears safe to assume that the northern territorial issue is potentially dangerous in that it is capable of arousing public passions.

More significant than the opinion of the public and the elite sector mentioned above is the basic position taken by the mass media and especially the national dailies (including *Asahi, Yomiuri,* and *Mainichi*). They appear to be unanimous in supporting the government's position, i.e., unless the return of all four islands is secured, a peace treaty with the Soviet Union should not be concluded. In interpreting the opinion data presented above, it is well to keep in mind that the press does not merely reflect the state of public opinion. Rather, the mass media themselves have had an important role in shaping that public opinion.

The issue is compounded by Japanese distrust and resentment of the Russians, especially for the latter's unilateral violation of the Neutrality Pact near the end of World War II (Oba, 1972: 62-63; Hanami, 1970; 40-41; Getsuyo Kai Repoto, 1969: 18-20). According to the *Jiji* press, which conducts a monthly opinion poll, the Soviet Union since 1960 has consistently been singled out by the largest proportion of the Japanese public as being the country most disliked. (The only exception was for a two-year period beginning in the latter half of 1966 extending through the first half of 1968).

An opinion poll conducted by the *Yomiuri* newspaper in June

1969 indicated that a nationwide sample of 3000 showed 42.9 percent disliking the Soviet Union, and only 2.9 percent liking it. (The United States fares better, with 23.9 percent liking it and 10.8 percent disliking it). The same poll showed the Soviet Union at the top of the list of countries posing the greatest threat to Japan's security, with 20 percent expressing this opinion.

The *Sankei* newspaper poll of October 1972, based on a sample of 1000 in the metropolitan areas of Tokyo and Osaka, showed similar results. The Soviet Union was nominated by 27.3 percent of the sample as the most disliked country, this segment being among the older population.

Another survey conducted by the Public Information Office of the Prime Minister to ascertain popular attitudes toward the United States, China, and the Soviet Union (based on a nation-wide sample of 3000) indicated 1.7 percent as liking and 27.2 percent as disliking the Soviet Union.

There are former residents of the Northern Territories and other groups agitating for the return of the islands, but they do not constitute an important political force, particularly as compared to the kind of pressure that was exerted for the reversion of Okinawa to Japan. They are, nevertheless, a force to be reckoned with, potentially powerful to the extent to which they are supported by the political parties and elite opinion as well as fishery interests.

The Japanese demand for the return of the Northern Territories was to a degree related to their demand for the reversion of Okinawa from the United States. The Japanese government felt it necessary and diplomatic, during the period of negotiation with the U.S. government, that it demonstrate a "proper" attitude by being equally insistent and anxious to recover the territories held by the Soviet Union. The current political leadership cannot wholly escape this legacy even today after the administrative rights over Okinawa have been returned to Japan.

The Japanese leaders may also have been conscious of the beneficial effect their position on this issue might have on Japan's relations with China, which has its own territorial claims with the Soviet Union. At any rate, having taken this stand, it is difficult for Japan to drop its territorial claims publicly without appearing to "betray" its Chinese friends.

The Japanese government feels that it must keep the issue alive, if only to prevent the Soviet government from justifying its control on the basis of uncontested rule (Sugiyama, 1973:1). Some Japanese perceive the issue as leverage against the Soviet Union to obtain concessions in other sectors, such as economic relations. This question will be dealt with later. Other Japanese entertain the hope that the Soviets may be compelled, in a major crisis such as a Sino-Soviet war, to return the islands in exchange for Japanese neutrality.

ECONOMIC DIMENSION: JAPAN'S COOPERATION IN SIBERIAN DEVELOPMENT PROJECTS

The Nature of the Projects

S ince the mid-1960s, negotiations relating to Japan's involvement in the development of Siberia have yielded some results. Agreements on three projects were concluded during 1968-1971: the timber agreement (July 1968); the agreement on the development of Vrangel port (December 1970); and the development of wood-chip and pulp production (December 1971).

Under the first agreement, Japan was to supply $133 million in equipment and $30 million in consumer goods over a three-year period for development of the timber and woodworking industry on the Amur River. Repayments were to be made in the form of Soviet exports of timber during 1969-1973. The terms of Japanese credit for the equipment were 20 percent deposit with repayment of the balance over a five-year period at 5.8 percent interest. Deferred payments were arranged on Japanese exports of $30 million in consumer goods.

The second project provided for Japanese delivery of equipment, machinery, and material for the development of Vrangel port in Eastern Siberia. Japanese credit of $80 million specified terms of 12 percent down and cash repayment in seven years at 6 percent interest.

The third agreement stipulated Japan's delivery of modern machinery and equipment for development of wood-chip and pulp production with deliveries to Japan for the period 1972-1981. Japanese credit of about $45 million was to be repaid over six years at a 6 percent interest rate.

Several projects have been under discussion between Japan and the Soviet Union. One is the development of heavy coking coal in south Yakutia for the 1974-1979 period. Preliminary information indicates that Japanese credit would be around $350 million with the Soviet Union, beginning in 1980, supplying about five million tons of coal. Another project would involve the exploitation of natural gas in Yakutia and its transportation through pipelines to the Soviet Far East. From there, LNG would be carried by tankers to Japan and the United States. Several alternative plans have been under discussion. Japan and the United States would provide a bank loan, with the Soviet Union delivering natural gas. At least 10 billion cubic meters of gas would be delivered annually both to Japan and to the United States. This project calls for construction on an area of minus 40 degrees centigrade with over 1500 feet of permafrost. In the summer of 1973, a memorandum was signed. A two-year survey will be financed by credits of $120 million to $150 million by Japan and the United States, with the terms of credit to be negotiated later. Japan would supply a bank loan of $1.7 billion for the project concurrent with the same amount of input from U.S. firms.

Other projects include Tyumen oil, prospecting oil and gas on the shelf of Sakhalin, development of Udokan copper ore and Buruktal nickel, as well as a second general agreement on the development of timber resources. The Tyumen project is considered by both sides to be the most important. For this project Japan would provide over a billion dollars in credit for pipe and other equipment to extend the existing pipeline from Tyumen to Irkutsk (4100 miles) and on to Nakhodka (2600 miles). Japan would be supplied with about 25 million tons of crude oil a year for 20 years.

The Soviet Desire for Japanese Involvement:
Economic Motivations

The Soviet Union needs Japan's capital and technology to accelerate the economic development of Siberia and the Soviet Far East. Under the 8th Economic Plan (1966-1970), it made heavy investments in the development of these areas. Special priority was placed on the establishment of industrial complexes in western Siberia. The 9th Plan, which expires in 1975, reflects Soviet intentions to proceed with the development of the eastern regions, with special emphasis on exploiting energy resources. The development of oil and gas resources and other industrial fuels in western Siberia is considered high in priority. As for eastern Siberia, emphasis is given to developing metallurgy and forestry resources and generating electric power. For the Far East, priority is on the development of the infrastructure related to power generation as well as mining, timber processing, construction of oil refineries, and the improvement of port facilities (Saeki, 1972: 213).

Several major objectives are discernible in these plans. The Soviet Union is determined to establish major economic complexes extending from European Russia to Siberia, utilizing local resources to provide industry with the necessary fuel and raw materials. The Soviets anticipate earning foreign currency and importing advanced machinery and consumer goods by exporting resources from Siberia. European Russia may be partially relied upon to assist in the development of western Siberia, but eastern Siberia and the Soviet Far East pose major problems in terms of transporting the necessary machinery, construction material, and consumer goods. This is what prompts the Soviets' desire to obtain these items from Japan. Economic cooperation with Japan would result in two major benefits: (1) stable markets for its resources, and (2) an opportunity to obtain the advanced technology vital to economic growth (Saeki, 1971: 3-4).

The Soviet economy has shown a noticeable downturn in growth rate in the 1960s, and it has been unable to improve labor productivity; therefore, the introduction of new technologies is critically needed. One of the characteristics of the current economic plan is the emphasis placed on technological progress. Through such progress, labor productivity would increase and a larger growth rate would follow.

Certain economic facts need to be kept in mind. In 1969, the production of crude oil in the Soviet Union was about 328 million tons, 70 percent of which came from west of the Urals.

At the 24th Party Congress in April 1971, the party leadership declared its intention to construct the largest petroindustrial base in western Siberia, and to develop gas supplies north of Tyumen. The focus of development, western Siberia, has an area of 2200 thousand sq. km. (about six times the size of Japan), encompassing the provinces of Tyumen and Tomsk. Oil resources are concentrated in the areas adjacent to the Ob river and its tributaries. Production of crude oil began in 1964, and the total reserve is estimated to be over 40 billion tons, with over 100 oil fields having been located to date. In 1964, the oil production along the banks of the Ob river reached 200,000 tons and has been increasing at a phenomenal rate since. The current economic plan projects 117 million tons by 1975, and the possibility of several hundred million tons by 1980 (Asahi Shimbun, 1972a, 1972e).

In 1970, oil demand in the Far East area of the U.S.S.R. was about 8 million tons, yet northern Sakhalin produced only 2.5 million tons. The remainder had to be transported by tank-car from Baikal on. Construction of a pipeline to Nakhodka would significantly reduce transportation costs, contributing toward the development of oil refineries and a petrochemical industry in the Far East, and also expediting the oil supply to the Soviet Pacific Fleet, merchant marine, and fishing vessels (Asahi Shimbun, 1972g). The Tyumen oil fields would provide 33 to 37 percent of total Soviet production by 1980. The Soviet Union does not have the vast funds necessary for the development of this infrastructure in the Far East.

Studies of Soviet publications are revealing for the kind of rationale advanced for Soviet-Japanese economic cooperation and the advantages foreseen for each side. Soviet sources have occasionally asserted that the Soviet Union is capable of implementing Siberian projects on a unilateral basis. For example, while the summit conference of October 1973 was in progress in Moscow, Tass (1973) reported a statement that the Soviet Union "of course, has the possibilities and means for solving this task by itself. But the U.S.S.R. has no intention of isolating itself from the rest of the world. If other countries show a desire to engage in economic cooperation with the U.S.S.R. on the basis of equality and mutual advantage . . . the Soviet Union is prepared to cooperate with them. And this fully applies to Japan". At the summit meeting, Brezhnev explained in detail the various Siberian development projects, but took no positive stand seeking the cooperation of Japan on the development of Tyumen oil and Yakutia natural gas resources. Rather, he indicated that Russia would not refuse if Japan agreed to cooperate in the development projects (FBIS, USSR, 1973a: M.9).

On the eve of the summit conference, *Izvestia* commentator Kudryavtsev (1973b) told Japanese correspondent Yoshinari of JOAK-TV, "The Soviet Union is capable of developing Siberia by itself, but we want mutual economic benefit". Writing in *Pravda*, V. Spandaryan (1971), member of the Soviet State Planning Committee, said that the Soviet Union is carrying out a policy of accelerated development of the productive forces in its eastern regions. The development of fuel, power, raw materials, and the industrial and agricultural resources of the Siberian area is "of serious national economic importance". More direct comment on the benefit of Japan's cooperation was made by Nikolai Nekrasov (1972), Soviet authority on Siberian development, in a talk during his visit to Japan in December 1972. He said that the Soviet Union gives highest priority to the Tyumen project and expects Japan and the United States to play a major role by extending their most advanced technology to Siberian development.

Evgeny S. Shershnev (1973), Deputy Director, Institute of U.S. Studies, identified several advantages the Soviet Union would derive from economic cooperation with Japan:

(1) specialization in exports to Japan would enable the Soviet Union to accelerate the development of her resources;

(2) overall expansion of trade with Japan would result through an involvement with the all-Union resources;

(3) the high technological level of Japanese industries would contribute to the acceleration of the rate of economic development of the Soviet Far East, and

(4) Broad opportunities would exist for the conclusion of large-scale transactions on a long-term basis.[7]

Several days preceding Tanaka's visit to the Soviet Union in October 1973, Moscow broadcast a series of commentaries on present and future U.S.S.R.-Japan trade and economic relations.

In the remarks of October 4 the following comments appeared, which offer an interesting economic rationale for both the Soviet Union and Japan (FBIS, USSR, 1973: M.3).

> One of the main Soviet tasks is to accelerate industrial production in Siberia and the Soviet Far East by developing abundant fuel and other natural resources and constructing a large-scale industrial belt there. The Soviet Union is fulfilling this task satisfactorily under the Ninth 5-year plan by using its own efforts and funds. However, we must fulfill the task more effectively and save time, funds and equipment. The best way to do so is to obtain bank credits from other countries to procure additional funds and equipment. Since Japan has no industrial (raw) materials even to fulfill its own domestic requirements, it is regarded as the most suitable country to offer bank credits to the Soviet Union.

> There is no hypocritical element in partnership between the Soviet Union and Japan. This partnership is based on the principle of providing mutual benefits, guaranteeing equality and reciprocally respecting each other's interests. If the Soviet Union is able to accelerate the development of natural resources through Japanese-offered bank credits, it will be given an opportunity not only to fulfill its domestic requirements but to produce more goods to repay the credits and expand its exports.

> As for Japan, the establishment of large-scale bases to supply fuel and other natural resources in Siberia and the Soviet Far East means the long-term and stable procurement of key raw materials. At present, the stable procurement of fuel and raw materials is of great importance throughout the capitalist world. Struggles for fuel resources are becoming more intense among capitalist countries.

> The cost of shipping fuel and other raw materials from Siberia to Japan is inexpensive because of their geographic proximity. If Japanese firms take part in the joint project for developing natural resources in Siberia and the Soviet Far East, Japan will be offered a promising and reliable sales market to sell its surplus industrial products.

The Soviet Desire for Japanese Involvement:
Political Considerations

According to some Japanese analysts (Asahi Shimbun, 1972e), one Soviet objective is to prevent or obstruct development of closer relations between Japan on the one hand and China and the United States on the other. Another suspected consideration is that the Soviet Union is having increased difficulty in meeting demands for oil emanating from abroad, especially Eastern Europe. Unless stability of supply is assured, Soviet influence over Eastern European countries would be weakened.

As these analysts see it (Asahi Shimbun, 1973f), the Soviet leaders are also haunted by the nightmare of an anti-Soviet coalition among Japan, the United States, and China. Japanese-Chinese normalization occurred with unanticipated speed, as did rapprochement between China and the United States. From the Soviet perspective, Japan's involvement in Siberian development would partially destroy the anti-Soviet coalition. By drawing Japan closer, the Soviet Union could move one step nearer the realization of a collective security system. It is significant, these analysts point out, that a Russian diplomat characterized Russo-Japanese cooperation in the development of Siberia as suggestive of the formation of a "Russo-Japanese Resource Alliance".

It may be difficult to substantiate the argument that China figures strongly in the Soviet decision to develop Siberia and the Soviet Far East. It is reasonable to assume, however, that the Soviet leaders have been acutely aware of the political and strategic implications of the development plans and Japan's role in them for Sino-Soviet relations, and for Japan's relationship with China.

Chinese sensitivity to Siberian projects will be discussed later. It is pertinent here to mention Soviet awareness of and sensitivity to Chinese views. To cite a few examples, on March 16, 1973, the Tass News Agency termed as "Chinese interference" Liao's observation that Tyumen oil may be utilized by the Soviet Union for military objectives against China. A Soviet newspaper carried a lengthy denunciation of Chinese objections to the Japanese-Soviet development of Tyumen, terming this "an intervention in the internal affairs of Japan" (Gaimusho Joho Bunka Kyoku, 1973: 48-59). Shortly after the summit conference in Moscow (October 1973), Askold Biryukov (1973), a Tass commentator, criticized China's alleged attempt to prevent rapprochement between the Soviet and Japanese peoples:

Before and during Premier Tanaka's visit to the U.S.S.R., the Maoists and their press were literally seized by anti-Soviet fever. In their
typical condescending manner, the Peking leaders ventured to
prompt the Japanese as to what they should and should not discuss
in Moscow. They were warned not to agree on cooperation with the
Soviet Union in the exploitation of Siberia's wealth, especially in
the construction of a trans-Siberian oil pipeline, because this "could
create a strategic problem for China".

... The Maoists clamped down upon the idea of building up a
collective security system in Asia. They thrust upon Japan their
advice not to renounce territorial claims. The Maoists still adhere to
this line in their attempts to prevent the rapprochement between
the Soviet and Japanese peoples.

It is reasonable to assume that the Soviet leaders are conscious
of the military implications in the development of Siberia. The
opening of the Tyumen oil fields and the construction of a
pipeline would play an important role in supplying oil requirements for Soviet ground forces on the Sino-Soviet borders and for
the Soviet Far Eastern Fleet. It is also reasonable to assume that
the Soviet leaders are aware of the leverage they would acquire
toward Japan. By being drawn economically closer, Japan might
be compelled to move closer politically to insure an adequate
return from her immense investment. In order to avoid Soviet
interruption of supplies, Japan might have to accommodate
Soviet wishes.

The Soviet leaders attach much importance to the *long-term*
character of the economic cooperation envisaged and show sensitivity to the political implications as well. As Semichastnov, First
Deputy Minister of Foreign Trade, indicated (1972a: 15-16,
1972b), the projects are intended to be carried out over a period
of 15 to 20 years and "the very fact they are long-range will help
to maintain and consolidate friendly, good-neighbor relations
between the U.S.S.R. and Japan."

The Soviet leaders are also aware of the implications of Japan's
extensive involvement vis-à-vis the United States. The close political, military, and economic ties between the United States and
Japan have long been a source of major Soviet concern. The
improved relations between the United States and the Soviet

Union during the past few years somewhat diminished the urgency and intensity of this concern over the U.S.-Japan Security Treaty, but the Soviet quest for its termination remains strong. The Soviet desire to reduce U.S.-Japanese politico-economic ties has also been indicated in Soviet publications since the "Nixon shocks" of July and August 1971. These contain frequent references to the alleged ever-growing contradictions between the United States and Japan. According to D. Petrov, a noted Soviet specialist on Japan, a sharp exacerbation of Japanese-American differences appeared in the second half of 1971, and is not restricted to trade and economic spheres. Divergence of opinion, he maintains, exists also over Japan's role in U.S. military strategy in Asia. Dr. Petrov (1972) writes:

> The acute differences between Washington and Tokyo on economic and military questions have also spread recently to the sphere of politics. A particularly broad response has been aroused in Japan by U.S. steps to repair relations with the PRC. The report on the Kissinger trip to Peking and on Nixon's upcoming visit there was taken in Tokyo as an underhanded blow—all the more palpable because it was inflicted unexpectedly and in the tenderest spot of Japanese diplomacy.

In the words of another writer (Ignatuschenko, 1972: 111-112), "the two biggest powers in the capitalist world are waging a bitter struggle for markets", and "the logic of imperialist economic rivalry leads one to expect that the American-Japanese contradictions will, if anything, grow deeper".

Another observer writes in *Pravda* (1972) that the latest American protectionist step has once again demonstrated, with utter clarity, the futility of the two rival countries' attempts to gloss over the incompatibility of their trade and economic interests. Writing in *Pravda*, Ovchinikov (1973) states that the problem of energy supplies is becoming more and more acute and the struggle over their sources is intensifying in the capitalist world. A clash between the United States and Japan would be fraught with serious consequences. He concludes by saying that "deep contradictions between the world's two largest imperial powers are far from being resolved".

The Japanese are reminded constantly of the folly and danger of excessive dependence upon and exclusive alliance with the United States. The Soviets applaud any developments indicating Japanese independence from the United States, and conflicts in policy, and seldom lose an opportunity to stress the availability of alternative ties with the Soviet Union. Propaganda for the expanding of trade and economic matters has been impressive. Numerous articles have appeared since the late 1960s, especially in the past few years, emphasizing complementary factors in the economic interests of the two countries.

In view of the avid interest the Soviet Union has shown in strained relations between the United States and Japan, it is reasonable to assume that the possible implications of Japan's extensive involvement in Siberian development has been a consideration for Soviet leaders. The deeper the extent to which Japan is drawn into the Siberian projects, the less exclusive will be her orientation toward the United States.

The Soviet Union initially favored bilateral cooperative arrangements with Japan from which the United States would be excluded, and has, on occasion, indicated a continued preference for this posture. It would be expected that the Soviet Union would attempt to play Japan and the United States against each other to increase its own bargaining position, as well as to explore alternatives, but the following considerations have tempered this course.

To begin with, for reasons to be explained later, the Japanese desire U.S. participation in Siberia in some form; in order for the Soviet Union to obtain Japanese government support, therefore, it must adhere to Japan's stipulation in this matter. Secondly, both the Soviet Union and Japan realize that in certain fields, such as construction under permafrost conditions and offshore drilling, the United States has the most advanced technology and experience to offer, and hence its participation in the technical field would be desirable.

The Soviet Union must believe that close economic cooperation would lead to general improvement in the relations between the two countries. The following passages by Kudryavtsev (1973a), which appeared in *Izvestia,* suggest this position:

> If enormous economic relations are created and if Japan benefits from them, psychological obstacles to Japan-Soviet cooperation will be gone ... economic cooperation already exists between our countries. ... But already this is insufficient, there is now talk of the joint working and exploitation of Tyumen oil, coking coal and gas in southern Yakutia. ... In short, the development of Soviet-Japanese relations at the present stage gives rise to the need for large-scale and long-term economic cooperation which will impart fresh scope and depth to Soviet-Japanese relations as a whole.

It may be an exaggeration to say that Soviet leaders expect the northern territorial issue to disappear entirely because of economic cooperation, but it is conceivable that they hope for a quiet de facto shelving of the issue. At the very least, the adamant intensity with which the northern territorial issue is pressed by the Japanese might be lessened. This interpretation has some valid basis and is certainly consistent with the Soviet belief that the northern territorial issue is really an artificial creation of the Japanese government. That belief is fed by another, that monopoly capital and business interests in fact determine Japanese government policy and that the Siberian development projects receive solid support from Japanese economic interests.

Soviet interpretation of Japan's interest in the Siberian development has been also visible in an analysis by V. Spandaryan (1971: 2), who contends that Japan has been experiencing increasing difficulty in its exports to capitalist countries, and that Japanese business and official circles are calling for a revision of Japan's "one-sided foreign economic orientation". According to Spandaryan, Japanese interest in trade and economic ties with the Soviet Union is "explained by economic necessity and corresponds to Japan's national interests."

In addition, an *Izvestia* article by Kudryavtsev of October 6, 1973, just prior to the summit conference, has the following passage:

> Political relations between countries become firm and stable when they rest on an equally firm and stable foundation of economic relations. This thesis fully applies to mutual relations between the U.S.S.R. and Japan. Japan, with its highly developed economy, depends greatly on imports of industrial raw material. ... It is well known that large foreign monopolies are not averse to taking advan-

tage of this weak side of the Japanese economy in order to try to influence certain aspects of Japanese policy. At the same time, "alongside" Japan we have the Soviet Union—this veritable storehouse of industrial raw material which has to explore and work its natural resources which have not yet been fully exploited.

He went on to say that no insuperable contradictions between the Soviet Union and Japan prevent fruitful, mutually beneficial cooperation, and pointed out that Japan would be dealing with the Soviet market, which is not subject to fluctuations.

Soviet leaders and commentators also point out that Japan's need for fuel and other resources is critical, suggesting that this matter should be of vital concern to the Japanese. They argue that in contrast the northern territorial issue is a nonissue or a minor artificial one, propagandized by revanchists and other forces interested in blocking improved relations between the countries. Russian comments have occasionally been more direct. They ask, "Which is more important to Japan's national interest, the Northern Territories or access to fuel and other resources?" From the perspective of this writer, the Russians tend to underestimate the intensity of Japan's desire for the return of the Northern Territories, while overemphasizing Japan's apparent need for access to Soviet resources.

The Soviet approach taken at the summit meeting appears consistent with this interpretation. As mentioned earlier, the remarks of Tanaka and Ohira that they would deal with the Siberian development issue as distinct from the northern territorial issue was welcome news to the Soviet leaders. At the summit conference of October 1973, Brezhnev spent two-and-a-half hours personally explaining the details of the Siberian development. This may accurately reflect Soviet priority on Siberian development and their desire for Japan's cooperation. Partly, at least, it may also reflect the Soviet strategy of diverting Japan from its campaign for the return of the Northern Territories.

The Soviet Union is aware that a peace treaty cannot be concluded easily because of the territorial issue. From the Soviet perspective it is desirable, in the absence of the peace treaty, to conclude a series of agreements that would have the cumulative effect of placing relations on a firmer foundation. For the conclusion of a treaty of friendship or a non-aggression pact, a conjunctive treaty of economic cooperation would be desirable for the Soviets. Each of these would represent to the Soviet Union a move toward "complete normalization" and the establishment of a collective security system for Asia. However, no treaties of this type were concluded at the summit conference of October 1973. From the Soviet perspective, however, the Joint Communiqué represented a firm commitment from the Japanese government to economic cooperation, including the development of Siberia and the Soviet Far East.

Factors Shaping Japan's Posture Toward Siberian Projects

What are the considerations that shape Japan's attitude toward participation in the Siberian development project? The most significant is the fact that the Japanese economy depends heavily upon a steady influx of imports of fuel and raw materials to sustain itself. Japan imports 99 percent of all the oil it consumes, and, given its low inventory capacity and ever-increasing need, the Japanese economy would be seriously damaged within a short time if the flow of oil were interrupted. Thus stability of supply is a primary goal—stability that is relatively immune from the vicissitudes of international politics and the international supply situation. The recent price offensive of the OPEC (Organization of Petroleum Exporting Countries) made Japan acutely aware that Arab sources could not be relied upon (Saeki, 1972: 4-5). Source diversification, therefore, is needed both to assure supply in view of the growing competition among industrialized nations and to avoid excessive dependence on any one source, thereby reducing the potential harm to the Japanese economy in the event of a supply interruption. Diversification is sought in terms of region, country, and political systems. Japan imports 86 percent of her petroleum from the Middle East and 12 percent from Southeast Asia. About 95 percent comes form OPEC countries— Iran, Saudi Arabia, Indonesia, and Kuwait are the largest suppliers—taking care of 80 percent of Japanese needs. Japan purchases crude oil primarily through foreign suppliers—59 percent from the major international suppliers (Exxon, Texaco,

Standard Oil of California, Mobil, British Petroleum, and Shell), 12 percent from independent U.S. oil companies, and 10 percent from Japanese suppliers (Albright, 1973: 3). For these reasons, Japan is especially alert for new sources of oil and sensitive to technological developments related to the extraction of oil and the process of reducing sulphur content.

Geographic proximity is an important factor affecting cost. Japan pays about $18 per ton for transporting coal from the United States, compared with about $3 a ton for transporting coal from the Soviet Far East. The Tyumen project would constitute an enormous saving in transportation. It takes Japan 29 days via 100,000-ton tanker and costs 1000 yen to transport a ton of crude oil from the Middle East. The cost from Nakhodka to Japan would be about one-fifth of this amount, and would take two days via tanker in the 25,000 to 50,000 class (Asahi Shimbun, 1973h). The Tyumen project would guarantee delivery of crude oil for 20 years, i.e., it meets the requirements of long-term supply. Moreover, the oil would have a low sulphur content. The sulphur content of Tyumen oil ranges from 0.9 to 1.6, and the oil shipped to Japan would have about a 1 percent sulphur content (Nihon Keizai Shimbun, 1972c).

As seen by the Japanese, their economy requires an expansion of export trade to sustain a high growth rate and to maintain a favorable balance of payments. They have duly noted the growth in the volume of Soviet foreign trade with non-Socialist countries and regard the Siberian development projects as a good opportunity to acquire access to the Soviet market (Saeki, 1972: 4). Under the Tyumen project, Japan would deliver pipe, equipment, and consumer goods, and the amount of trade turnover would be greatly increased. Japanese-Soviet trade has been on the increase since the mid-1950s and in 1973 reached a high of $1,562 million. Japanese exports came to $484 million, while imports totaled $1,078 million. In a meeting in February, Soviet and Japanese trade officials agreed further to expand bilateral trade, and this year Japan's exports to the Soviet Union are expected to increase 50 percent over the 1973 level. The increase will center on machinery, iron and steel products, chemical goods, textiles, and textile products (FBIS, USSR, 1974: M.2).

In addition to economic considerations, Japanese leaders are conscious of the political implications of closer economic cooperation with the Soviet Union. They feel that Japan would obtain leverage vis-à-vis the Soviet Union, China, and the United States. Japan's cooperation would provide a bargaining point against the Soviet Union on political questions, possibly including the northern territorial question. The improved relations accompanying massive economic interdependency might provide more opportunity for possible resolution of the matter.

Regarding other political considerations, the Japanese are aware of the effect Japanese-Soviet economic cooperation would have on China. The Japanese government's serious move toward the Siberian development project came after the normalization of Japanese-Chinese relations. Japanese leaders sense enormous Soviet distrust and suspicion that Japanese-Chinese collusion against the Soviet Union might be taking place. Having arrived at a better understanding with China, the Japanese leaders feel the need to maintain a balance by improving relations with the Soviet Union. In view of Tanaka's decline in popularity in Japan, Japanese-Soviet relations seem to provide a potentially meaningful demonstration of his leadership.

A movement toward the Soviet Union in the economic sphere would also serve as a countervailing force vis-à-vis China and the United States. At the same time, of course, the Japanese are aware that their massive involvement in the Siberian projects would also make Japan vulnerable to Soviet pressure. She might upon occasion be compelled to take the Soviet side against China or the United States, if only to protect her investments and assure the continued delivery of oil and raw materials.

On the other hand, Japanese leaders have been sensitive to Chinese views on Japanese-Soviet economic cooperation. The Chinese have on numerous occasions expressed concern with the Tyumen project in particular. In January 1973, Chou En-lai warned Nakasone, Japanese Minister of Trade and Industry, against relying on the Soviet Union for resources, saying that Chinese experience had taught them the Russians are not to be trusted. He said he was opposed to the Tyumen project, as it would strengthen the Soviet armed forces in the Far East. On March 10, 1973, Liao, a Chinese official, told a group of *Yomiuri* reporters that China did not oppose friendly relations between

Japan and the Soviet Union and that China appreciated the importance of resources to Japan; however, the Tyumen project would enable the Soviet Union to supply fuel for its tanks and planes for an invasion of China, and China would be forced to take preventive measures. Chinese feeling would be aroused and that would be of greater consequence than the commotion over divorce if Japan were to give the Soviet Union material assistance (Nihon Keizai Shimbun, 1972d). More recently, Premier Chou told a Japanese business leader, Uemura, on September 5, 1973, that it would be wise for Japan to have the United States participate in the Siberian development, but asked Uemura to consider seriously the impact this development project would have on China (Asahi Shimbun, 1973a).

As of January 1972, the Japanese Foreign Ministry was cautious toward the Tyumen project. Several considerations were operative—one was that Japan's involvement might have an adverse effect on chances for normalizing her relations with China, another was that the project would indirectly strengthen Soviet military capability, certainly provoking China. Moreover, the strengthening of Soviet forces would heighten Japan's concern with her own security. Japan could not be expected immediately to endorse the idea of relying on the Soviet Union for such a vital resource as oil.

The Japanese government subsequently approved in principle the use of an Export-Import Bank loan to finance the Tyumen project, yet decided against the extension of Export-Import Bank credit in relation to the construction of a refinery at Nakhodka. It held that the 200 million dollars needed for refinery construction must come from private sources. Two major reasons governed this decision. First, the idea of constructing a refinery represented a fundamental modification of the original Tyumen project as discussed with the Japanese government. Secondly, Japan's use of government funds would further alienate China, which would view the project as further enhancing Soviet military capability, and would be inconsistent with Japan's own preferred policy of "equidistance" (Asahi Shimbun, 1973c). The Japanese government itself realized that a refinery would facilitate fuel supply to the Soviet Pacific Fleet and would provide the Soviet Union with a unilateral advantage. As Uemura (1973) put it in his address to a group of LDP leaders on July 26, 1973, the Siberian development project is important for a nation deficient in natural resources, but Japan should preserve "equal distance" between the Soviet Union and China to prevent the Siberian issue from provoking a Sino-Soviet border dispute.

Another question shaping Japan's attitude toward Siberian development is whether or not U.S. firms would participate. U.S. participation is desirable from the Japanese standpoint to lessen China's leverage and her fear of Soviet-Japanese collusion against her. Initially, Japanese business leaders were not enthusiastic about U.S. participation, and as of January 1972, Imazato was determined to carry out the Tyumen project without it (Asahi Shimbun, 1972f). At that time, he thought that Japan could borrow part of the funds from private firms. By mid-1972, however, the idea of bringing U.S. firms into certain key projects was being seriously entertained. The Bechtel Corporation was asked for technical assistance in the Tyumen project because of its technological expertise in the construction of pipeline and port facilities (Nihon Keizai Shimbun, 1972b). At about the same time, the Gulf Oil Company exhibited an interest in the Tyumen project, offering to defray part of the several billion dollars Japan would have to advance to the Soviet Union in return for crude oil. The basic general contract, however, would be signed by Japan and the Soviet Union. Gulf's possible participation was welcomed by Japanese leaders, including all relevant government ministries. By this time, the involvement of the United States was being regarded as advantageous on a number of grounds:

(1) it would eliminate U.S. objections to the project on the theory that it would unilaterally benefit the Soviet Union;

(2) it would help Japan in maintaining good relations with China, in view of the U.S.-Chinese détente. China's objection to Japanese involvement in the Siberian development projects would be blunted, and she would be less likely to suspect Japanese-Soviet collusion (Asahi Shimbun, 1972d); and

(3) it would enable Japan to share financial risks—the Tyumen project alone would require over one billion dollars of credit, and the aggregate credit for the several projects would be about five billion dollars.

In view of its potential impact on China alone, U.S. participation was fast becoming a contingency of Japanese involvement (Nihon Keizai Shimbun, 1972a; Asahi Shimbun, 1972b). By June 1972, Imazato was saying that he was considering a three-nation joint project with the Gulf Oil Company participating in the Tyumen and the other projects as well (Asahi Shimbun, 1972c).

An international development also prompted a change of heart on the part of Japanese businessmen. Since the Nixon-Brezhnev meeting in May 1972, U.S. participation had also become acceptable to the Soviet Union; in fact they began actively negotiating the possibility of joint development with U.S. firms. The Soviet Union went so far as to propose the Yakutia project to the El Paso Natural Gas Company while it was still under discussion between the Japanese and the Soviet Union (Asahi Shimbun, 1972b).

Still another factor affecting Japan's acceptance of the Tyumen project was the terms of agreement under which Japan would participate. Two commercial issues deserve special mention, the first concerning credit terms and the other purchase assurance. The Soviet Union had insisted on financing through bank loans instead of using suppliers' credit, as had been done in such earlier projects as the timber contract, thereby hoping for maximum Japanese government participation and minimum interest charges. The Soviets would have to negotiate the bank loan portion of the financing at prevailing commercial rates, but with an involvement of the Japanese government, it could keep the commercial portion as low as possible by financing a substantial amount through government credit agencies (Albright, 1973: 16-18).

Despite Soviet persistence on the matter of the bank loans and government guarantee of the purchase of delivered goods, the Japanese government had by early 1973 still made no firm commitment. It would promise only to give positive, favorable consideration to such matters when the agreements had been reached at private level.

The preliminary Japanese decision to give government support for the Tyumen project came on February 28, 1973, when government agencies, including the Foreign Ministry, approved the use of bank loans. Up to this point, the predominant government view was cautious, since it was thought that the Tyumen project constituted a threat to China. The government feared Japan's influence on the Soviet Union would be weakened by seeking a Soviet oil supply; more importantly, if the government proceeded with economic cooperation, it might be taken as de facto abandonment of the northern territorial issue at a time when the Soviet Union had made no concessions (Nihon Keizai Shimbun, 1973b). The reassessment of the position of the Foreign Ministry was attributed to the following considerations. First, Japan's participation in the Tyumen project would have no major adverse impact on the nation's security, nor would it significantly weaken Japan's voice toward the Soviet Union. Second, Japanese-Soviet economic cooperation in which the United States was partially involved would not introduce an unstable element in Japan's relations with China or Japan's diplomacy in Asia. This assessment was also reinforced by the view that the evolving American-Chinese relations and Japanese-Chinese normalization have placed Soviet diplomacy in a very difficult situation and that Japan's refusal to take part in the Tyumen project would alienate the Soviet Union, possibly inducing instability in the Asian situation (Nihon Keizai Shimbun, 1973b).

It must be pointed out that the positions taken by the Japanese government agencies on the Tyumen question varied. The Ministry of Trade and Industry and the Ministry of Finance had been more favorably disposed than the Foreign Ministry. As early as March 1972, the Ministry of Finance came out in support of the project. It announced that it would allow a one-billion-dollar bank loan for the Tyumen project, provided the Foreign Ministry and Ministry of Trade and Industry anticipated no diplomatic or technical difficulties in the project. Two factors appear to have shaped this decision: first, it would more effectively use foreign reserves, which had passed the level of $16 billion; second, now that the Soviet side made available specific data on the Tyumen project, the undertaking appeared more realistic (Asahi Shimbun, 1972f).

On June 21, 1972, Prime Minister Tanaka announced that the

government would approve the use of Export-Import Bank funds for the Tyumen project and that the government would provide assurance that Japan would purchase the oil delivered (Asahi Shimbun, 1973e). Following the Nixon-Tanaka meeting in which cooperation between Japan and the United States on Siberian development was agreed upon, the Japanese government appeared willing to underwrite one-third of the funds needed for Siberian projects. The estimate given at that time (August 2, 1973) was $5 billion. The Japanese government would approve a government loan of up to $1.7 billion, provided U.S. and Japanese private firms concluded satisfactory cooperative arrangements (Asahi Shimbun, 1973d).

On October 10 the Japanese government, in the form of a Japanese-Soviet Joint Communiqué, made a definite commitment to support the Siberian development projects. More specifically, Tanaka agreed that when the Tyumen and other projects were concluded by agreement of private firms with their Soviet counterparts the government would begin to negotiate to elevate these private agreements to governmental level (Nihon Keizai Shimbun, 1973a).

Yet another major factor favoring Japanese participation in the Siberian projects was the positive attitude expressed by Japanese industrial and business groups. The highly interdependent relationship between government and business in Japan makes political leaders particularly susceptible to business preferences. For example, one businessman, Nagano, called upon Foreign Minister Ohira to practice separation of political and economic principles, urging Ohira not to use the Siberian proposal as a lever for the northern territorial issue. The desire for early resolution of the development question on the part of business circles is a factor Japanese political leaders cannot ignore. This is not to deny that the Japanese government has provided "guidance" for the business circles throughout the negotiations on the Siberian projects. There has been a close working relationship, and the government leadership has on the whole served as a sobering and cautionary influence.

When the summit conference was concluded in October 1973, Mr. Imazato was reported to have exclaimed that the business community may have been relieved of the issue of economic cooperation. It had become politicized; that is to say, it had become intertwined with the northern territorial issue. This sentiment was shared by other members of the business community until a Foreign Ministry official and Tanaka urged business leaders to proceed with the conclusion of agreements on the projects regardless of progress made on the territories.

PART IV

THE FUTURE OF JAPANESE-SOVIET RELATIONS

I n considering the range of Japan's alternative security arrangements, it is not entirely unrealistic to suggest the possibility of a Japanese-Soviet alliance. Many developments in recent years appear to warrant an assessment of this possibility. For example, some observers consider that U.S. policies pursued in the name of the Nixon Doctrine, the "Nixon shocks" of July and August 1971, the evolving relations between the United States and China, and the oil crisis are impelling Japan to move closer to the Soviet Union.

In the judgment of this author, such a development is highly unlikely and would occur only under an extraordinary combination of several circumstances:

A major realignment of domestic political forces. The ruling LDP must not only lose majority control of both Houses of the Diet, but must also be relegated to an insignificant parliamentary group as well. This factor is highly unlikely during the period under study. A coalition government (a remote possibility), whether led by the LDP or the JSP, would not seek defense ties with the Soviet Union unless an external development posing a major military threat were to occur. There are no significant political forces in Japan now that would seek military alliance with the Soviet Union, nor are any likely to emerge in the near future.

A radical reorientation and restructuring of existing patterns of trade and economic ties. These current patterns constitute a major constraint on strategic political choices. No Japanese leader, regardless of differences in ideology, could remain insensitive to the realities of economic life nor ignore the economic consequences of political decisions.

A sharp decrease in the profound distrust that the Japanese have for the Soviet Union. Opinion polls have consistently demonstrated that the Japanese dislike the Soviet Union more than almost any other country in the world. Japanese distrust of the Soviet Union is pervasive. Both the Soviet Union's unilateral abrogation of the Neutrality Pact toward the end of World War II and the continued Soviet occupation of the Northern Territories evoke intense resentment. It is possible that Japanese public opinion could undergo a significant change during the period under study, but this assumes Japan's decisive estrangement from the United States and the anticipation of major external threats emanating from non-Soviet sources.

A significant deterioration in Japanese relations with the United States and/or China. Japan would have to foresee a military threat from one of these countries and have her security ties with the United States severed. It is possible, and indeed probable, that in the years ahead, American-Japanese relations will undergo severe stress as the reliability of the security treaty diminishes in Japan's eyes. There are a number of existing and potential sources of discord. However, these do not justify an assumption of the development of hostile relations between Japan and the United States during the period under consideration.

In any speculation on future relations between Japan and the Soviet Union in the relatively near future, the following observations seem warranted:

1. The northern territorial issue will not be resolved, but will remain a fundamental impediment to major improvement in the political relations between the two countries. Japan will not sign a peace treaty or nonaggression pact that would imply Japan's abandonment of its claim to the islands. Similarly, Japan will remain opposed to the Soviet version of a collective security system, inasmuch as Japan's participation in this system would be tantamount to her acceptance of present borders. Since China opposes the collective security system, Japan will also make this an operative factor in her desire to avoid Chinese alienation.

2. Japan will participate in most of the Siberian development

projects that have been under discussion. The Tyumen project will encounter rough sailing, however.

3. Japan's awareness of the political implications in closer economic ties with the Soviet Union and her sensitivity to dependence on the Soviet Union for her supplies of critical fuel and raw materials will continue to induce a cautious attitude, imposing an effective upper limit to her economic entanglement in this area.

4. Japan will struggle to pursue a policy of equidistance and balance of power between the Soviet Union and China, and gradually toward the United States as well. She will become more assertive and independent vis-à-vis the United States, but despite occasional strains between the two countries, the nature of economic, political, and security ties will not be fundamentally altered.

EPILOGUE

The preceding chapters of this book, essentially completed in early March 1974, cover developments in Soviet-Japanese relations to the end of February. This epilogue is intended as an afterword, adding a brief discussion of the latest Soviet proposal on the Tyumen project.

In late March 1974, the Japanese were surprised by a major change in Soviet plans regarding the Tyumen project. The Soviets proposed the construction and use of a new trans-Siberian railroad for transporting Tyumen oil for Japanese use, rather than their original idea of a pipeline. Brezhnev and Kosygin made this proposal to Uemura and Nagano, visiting Japanese business leaders, and solicited Japan's cooperation in the construction of the new railway.

The revised Soviet proposal caused consternation in Japan. In the eyes of the Japanese, it represented a major and a fundamental modification of the original Tyumen project. Japan's participation in the building of the new railway system appears to them preposterous, since it would greatly enhance Soviet military and industrial capabilities. The proposal reinforced Japan's sensitivity to Chinese opinion, which would now be expected to intensify in opposition to Japan's involvement in the Tyumen project. The Japanese are also concerned with possible major strains in Japanese-U.S. relations.

The Japanese press, including such major dailies as *Asahi, Mainichi,* and *Yomiuri,* was nearly unanimous in expressing profound reservations, and in urging caution in Japan's participation in the project. All major newspapers shared in the assessment that the Tyumen proposal can no longer be considered as only an economic undertaking but has assumed politico-military and strategic dimensions as well. They contended that Japan should protect her relations with the U.S. and China, both of whom might be adversely affected by Japan's involvement in the railway project. It was clear that the suggestion added fresh impetus to Japanese distrust of the Russians.

The attitude of the Japanese government toward the Tyumen proposal has become more cautious than it was previously. This caution is due to two factors in particular: (1) sensitivity to probable Chinese opposition, and (2) awareness of U.S. uncertainty of, and probable nonparticipation in, the Siberian development projects. Prime Minister Tanaka himself expressed the belief that the modified project would have a bearing on Japan's national security, advising business leaders to take a cautious attitude. At a parliamentary committee session, Foreign Minister Ohira remarked that Japan's participation should occur "under the circumstance that other countries, such as China, understand Japan's action".

Under the new Soviet proposals, oil would presumably be transported through the existing pipeline from Tyumen to the Irkutsk area. It would then be carried eastward by the proposed railway. The new line, to be called BAM (Baikal-Amur Mainline) would commence at Ustkut north of Lake Baikal and would extend to Komsomolsk-Na-Amure. (In addition to the existing trans-Siberian railway, there is a railway to Ustkut—it branches off at Taishet west of Irkutsk.) From that point, a pipeline would be used to carry crude oil to Nakhodka. Alternative points, other than Nakhodka, may be selected and a railway used. There is an existing line between Komsomolsk-Na-Amure on the one hand and Khavarovsk and Sovetskaya Gavani on the other.

A more detailed treatment of Japan's misgivings and skepticism regarding the new proposal is given below:

1. Is it technically possible to transport 25 million tons of crude oil per year by the proposed railway? According to a Japanese estimate, to provide Japan with this quantity four separate runs would have to be made daily by a freight train consisting of 100 cars through regions which suffer from extreme climatic conditions for over half the year.

2. Aside from the question of technical feasibility, would it be economical for Japan to participate under the new terms? The amount of the bank loan the Soviets are requesting has been increased to $3.2 billion from the initial amount of approximately one billion dollars. The loan appears to the Japanese to be a large sum for Japan to assume single-handedly, and the necessity for diffusion of risk is thus greater than before. The amount of crude oil delivery (25 million tons) appears small in relation to

the total bank loan involved. Moreover, the Japanese are told that the maximum level of 25 million tons will not be attained until 1985.

3. In view of the increment in Soviet industrial capacity, especially military capability, which the construction of the railway would enhance, would Japan's participation affect her relations with the United States adversely and, in particular, would Japanese-U.S. security arrangements be jeopardized?

4. The enhancement of Soviet military capability would pose a security problem for Japan and the question remains as to why Japan should assist the Soviet Union in increasing that capability.

5. Japan's relations with China would be strained. Furthermore her policy of equidistance vis-à-vis the Soviet Union and China would be jeopardized. What effect would Japan's involvement have on the Sino-Soviet conflict?

6. The Japanese suspect that the Soviet move was motivated in part by its political objective of containing China and driving a wedge between Japan on the one hand and the United States and China on the other. This induces caution.

7. The Japanese are not certain how their participation would affect the settlement of the territorial dispute. Press commentaries on this subject are scarce; one view holds that the more extensive Japanese economic involvement and concomitant political cordiality, the greater is the possibility of Soviet concessions, owing to the decreasing politico-strategic value of the islands to the Soviet Union. A contrary view holds that Japan's deep involvement means the relinquishment of her economic leverage in relation to the Northern Territories.

The Japanese reactions outlined above were received by the Soviets with a sense of regret and exasperation. Upon learning of Japan's negative response, the Soviets attempted to underplay the extent to which they had anticipated Japanese participation. The Soviet attitude since then has been that she does not expect Japan to participate directly in the construction of the railway, and that the Soviet Union would merely use a portion of Japanese credit for that equipment and facilities related to, and required for, rail transportation of crude oil to Japan. The Japanese claim to have received contradictory signals from the

Soviet Union, and are convinced that the Soviet Union expects direct Japanese participation in the building of the railway itself.

The Soviets have reiterated the view that the Soviet Union will construct the railway independently, and that they are only interested in the use of a portion of Japanese credit for the purchase of the equipment and material necessary for rail transportation of crude oil to Japan. They argue that the idea of constructing a second trans-Siberian railway had long been under consideration but that it had been delayed because of economic considerations. If constructed, the railway could transport not only oil but other resources, such as coal and timber, and this should also be beneficial and acceptable to Japan. The Soviet Ambassador to Japan, O. Troyanovsky, remarked that Japan's contention that the construction of a railroad would enhance Soviet military capability is absurd, reflecting cold-war mentality and conceptions prevalent at the beginning of this century. He contended that the Soviet Union could construct the railway alone, and indeed presently has it under construction. Completion is expected in five years. Despite these assertions, the Japanese remain skeptical as to the wisdom of Japan's participation in this adaptation of the Tyumen project.

A protocol covering the financial arrangements for the following three projects was signed on April 22, 1974: South Yakutia coking coal, Yakutsk natural gas and forestry resources. The loan will be rendered in yen with most of the equipment and material to be purchased from Japan. The grace period will extend from 5 to 8 years. The amount of the bank loan from Japan will be $450 million in yen for the coking coal project, $100 million in yen for the natural gas project and about $500 million in yen for the timber project. The interest rate for the loan will be 6.375 per annum with a 10 percent downpayment on each project. The protocol would become effective if the general agreements on the three projects are concluded within 6 months after its signing.

A memorandum on the joint development of coking coal deposits in South Yakutia was signed on April 23, 1974. The Soviet Union will use a $450 million bank loan to purchase mining and railroad construction equipment and will export to

Japan 3,200,000 tons of Neryungra coking coal in 1983, 4,260,000 tons in 1984, and 5,500,000 tons annually from 1985 through 1998. The agreement also provides that the Soviet Union will export to Japan one million tons of Kuznetsk coking coal yearly from 1979 through 1998 in addition to the existing ordinary amount of trade between the two countries. If current trade is included at its peak period, the annual import of coking coal to be exported to Japan under the agreement is expected to reach 104,460,000 tons.

Another memorandum was signed on April 26 on the Yakutsk natural gas development project but it will not be complete without U.S. participation. Two years of exploration will be conducted and if the projected one trillion cubic meters of natural gas resources is confirmed, the project would be initiated so as to provide Japan and the United States each with 10 billion cubic meters annually for 25 years. Initially a bank loan from Japan and the United States totalling $200 million would be extended, and Japan has already made a commitment to provide $100 million. The Soviet Union is seeking an eventual total amount of about $3.5 billion to build a 1500 mile pipeline to the coast and a gas liquefaction plant.

On April 26 a memorandum was also signed on joint exploration of oil and natural gas on the continental shelf off Sakhalin. It included the following provisions: Japan will supply $100 million credit for the initial 5-year period for exploration. If the prospecting is successful, the Soviet Union will repay the credit at 6 percent interest primarily in the form of oil during the 18 years following the start of prospecting. The Japanese Petroleum Development Corporation or another firm will provide an additional $20 to $25 million loan for Soviet purchase of equipment, such as computers and other items necessary for exploration. An additional $30 million loan will be supplied by Japan for local expenses such as personnel, and related expenditures. Japan will also provide 50 percent of the necessary funds when the prospecting reaches the developmental stage. The Soviet Union will not object to the participation of U.S. firms as partners of Japan.

NOTES

1. For Soviet views on Japan in English, see Pavlovsky (1972, 1969); Latyshev (1972); Zakharov (1972); Sladkovsky (1970); Vasilyev (1969); Petrov (1968, 1965b); and Dalnov (1966). For a discussion of Soviet views on Japan's defense policy and on Soviet strategy, see Spahr (1973).

2. For a discussion of Soviet foreign policy, see Kosaka (1973) and Yano (1973). See also Shishikura (1972); Harako (1973, 1972); and Asahi Shimbun Anzen Hosyo Mondai Chosa Kai (1967b).

3. For a commentary on the NPT, see Kotani (1968).

4. For Japanese interpretations of U.S. policy toward China, see the special issue on American-Chinese relations of Azia Kuotari (1972). See also articles in the October, 1971, issue of Kokusai Jihyo by Ishikawa, Kosaka, Kamiya, Iriye, and Kotani.

5. For a brief history of the Kuriles, see Yamamoto (1951) and Hashimoto (1973).

6. In his memoirs, Matsumoto writes that when Kono told Ishikov for the second time that Japan wanted immediate return of Habomai, Ishikov asked whether he could interpret Japan's proposal to mean that the territorial problem would not be discussed later and that the territorial problem would not be raised at the time a peace treaty was concluded. It is intriguing that Matsumoto did not record the Japanese response.

7. Chinese concern with Japanese-Soviet talks can be seen by the manner in which the NCNA reported on the issue of the Northern Territories after the Japanese-Soviet summit meeting. The Chinese cited Japanese newspapers' accounts, giving the issue prominent coverage.

REFERENCES

Akahata (1971) May 20.

ALBRIGHT, R. (1973) "Siberian energy for Japan and the United States." Fifteenth Session, Senior Seminar in Foreign Policy, U.S. Department of State, 1972-1973.

AMANO, R. (1969) "Rikujo jieitai no gensei to mondaiten." pp. 58-65 in Nihon no Anzen Hoshyo Henshu Iinkai (ed.) Jieitai Ron.

Asahi Shimbun (1973a) October 13.

--- (1973b) October 11.

--- (1973c) September 9.

--- (1973d) August 3.

--- (1973e) June 22.

--- (1973f) May 12.

--- (1972a) December 12.

--- (1972b) June 17.

--- (1972c) June 15.

--- (1972d) May 28.

--- (1972e) April 22.

——— (1972f) March 4.

——— (1972g) February 21.

——— (1972h) February 9.

——— (1972i) January 6.

Asahi Shimbun Anzen Hoshyo Mondai Chosa Kai (1967a) Nihon no Jieiryoku. Tokyo: Asahi Shimbun Sha.

——— (1967b) Soren Gaiko to Azia.

Azia Kuotari (1972) "Beichu kankei no shin dankai to Nippon." (January).

BALLIS, W.B. (1964) "A decade of Soviet-Japanese relations." Studies on the Soviet Union, Vol. III, #3.

BIRYUKOV, A. (1973) Statement quoted in FBIS, USSR (October 19): M.3.

Chosa Geppo (1973) "Betonamu sengo no bei chu so no Azia seisaku." (June).

——— (1972) "Soren kaigun ryoku no zokyo to gaiyo shinshutsu." (October).

——— (1969a) "Soren naigai seisaku no mondai ten." (September).

——— (1969b) "Kunashiri, Etorofu ryoto no ryoyuken mondai." (Naikaku Chosa Shitsu) May.

Current Digest of Soviet Press (1970) December 22.

——— (1964) October 14.

Dal'nii Vostok (1968) No. 1.

DALNOV, V. (1966) "Japan's role in the U.S. aggression." New Times (July 13).

Department of State Bulletin (1956) Vol. XXXV, No. 900 (September 24).

DULLES, J.F. (1951) Statement in Department of State Bulletin Vol. XXIV, No. 614 (April 9).

FBIS, USSR (1974) February 25.

——— (1973a) October 9.

——— (1973b) October 5.

Gaimusho (1973) Tanaka Sori Daijin no Sorempo Homon (October).

Getsuyo Kai Repoto (1969) Hoppo Ryodo no Sho Mondai (December 22).

HANAMI, T. (1970) "Hoppo zen ryodo ga Nihon ryo da." Seikai Orai (January): 40-41.

HARAKO, R. (1973) "Peking-Mosukuwa kyofu no kinko." Keizai Orai (June): 74-85.

——— (1972) "Soren naigai seisaku no mujun." Jiyu (October): 44-53.

HARRISON, J.A. (1953) Japan's Northern Frontier. Gainsville: University of Florida Press.

HASHIMOTO, R.T. (1973) "The Northern Territories as an issue of national interest in Soviet-Japanese Relations." M.A. Thesis. Washington, D.C.: George Washington Univ.

HAYES, R. (1972) The Northern Territorial Issue. Arlington, Va.: Institute for Defense Analysis.

HELLMANN, D.C. (1969) Japanese Foreign Policy and Domestic Politics. Berkeley: Univ. of California Press.

HIRANO, Y. (1972) "Saikin no nisso kankei." Azia Kuotari Vol. 4, No. 3 (July).

Hoppo Ryodo Fukki Kisei Domei (1967) Hoppo Ryodo no Shomondai. Tokyo: Hoppo Ryodo Fukki Kisei Domei.

IGNATUSHCHENKO, S. (1972) Article in International Affairs (February 21).

International Affairs (1964) October.

International Institute for Strategic Studies (1974) The Military Balance, 1973-1974. London: International Institute for Strategic Studies.

ISHIKAWA, T. (1971) Article in Kokusai Jihyo (October).

Izvestia (1972) February 4.

——— (1970a) Article (November 13) in Current Digest of Soviet Press, Vol. XXII, No. 46 (December 15).

——— (1970b) Article (November 13).

——— (1970c) Article (October 20).

Japanese Ministry of Foreign Affairs (1970) Northern Territorial Issue. Tokyo.

Japan Report (1970) "Solution of northern territorial issue pressed." (December 16).

KAMIYA, F. (1971) Article in Kokusai Jihyo (October).

KHRUSHCHEV, N. (1966) Letter (December 8, 1961) quoted on pp. 235-236 of Nampo Doho Engo Kai, Hoppo Ryodo Mondai Shiryo Shu. Tokyo: Nampo Doho Engo Kai.

Komei Shimbun (1973) July 29.

KOSAKA, M. (1973) "Soren no Azia seisaku." Azia Kuotari (January-March): 98-104.

——— (1971) Article in Kokusai Jihyo (October).

KOTANI, H. (1971) Article in Kokusai Jihyo (October).

——— (1968) "Kaku kakusan boshi joyaku no imi suru mono." pp. 21-50 in Nihon no Anzen Hosho Henshu Iinkai (ed.) Kaku Jidai to Nihon no Kaku Seisaku.

Krasnaya Zvezda (1970) October 20.

KUDRYAVTSEV, V. (1973a) Article in Izvestia (October 6) published in FBIS, USSR (October 10): M.5.

——— (1973b) Television interview (October 6).

——— (1970) Article in Izvestia (November 13).

LATYSHEV, L. (1972) "Okinawa." International Affairs (March): 63-67.

MAEHARA, M. (1962) "Hoppo ryodo no hoteki chii" in Y. Shien (ed.) Hoppo Ryodo no Chii. Tokyo: Nampo Doho Engo Kai.

Mainichi Shimbun (1973a) October 13.

——— (1973b) October 12.

——— (1973c) October 11.

MATSUMOTO, S. (1970) Northern Territories and Russo-Japanese Relations. Hokkaido: Japanese League for the Return of the Northern Territories.

——— (1966) Mosukuwa ni Kakeru Nizi. Tokyo: Asahi Shimbun Sha.

Mirovaya Economika i Mezhdunarodnyye Otnosheniy (1968) No. 2.

MIYAUCHI, K. (1972) "Soren no Azia shudan ampo koso." Kokusai Jihyo (July): 44-49.

MIYOSHI, O. (1972) "Soren Azia seisaku no shin tenkai." Komei (June): 66-71.

MURTHY, P.A.N. (1964) "The Kurile Islands in Japan's relations with the Soviet Union." India Quarterly (July-September).

Nampo Doho Engo Kai (1966) Hoppo Ryodo Mondai Shiryo Shu. Tokyo: Nampo Doho Engo Kai.

NEKRASOV, N. (1972) Reported in Asahi Shimbun (December 12).

New Times (1964) "A.I. Mikoyan on Soviet-Japanese relations." (June 10).

Nihon Keizai Shimbun (1973a) (October 11).

——— (1973b) (March 1).

——— (1973c) (February 24).

——— (1972a) (May 30).

——— (1972b) (May 24).

——— (1972c) (February 24).

——— (1972d) (January 2).

Nihon Shakaito Senkyo Taisaku Iinkai (1972) So Senkyo Seisaku Shu.

NISHIMURA, T. (1969) "Kaijo jieitai no gensei to mondai ten." in Nihon no Anzen Hosho Henshu Iinkai (ed.) Jieitai Ron.

NOTO, E. (1971) Minzoku no Higan. Tokyo: Kokusai Shoko Rengo.

OBA, S. (1972) "Fuho senyu sareta hoppo ryodo." Seikai Orai (June): 62-68.

OVCHINIKOV, V. (1973) Article in Pravda (August 4).

PAVLOVSKY, V. (1972) "Collective security." International Affairs (July): 23-27.

——— (1969) "Problems of regionalism in Asia." International Affairs (April).

PETROV, D. (1968) "Japan in U.S. strategy." International Affairs (June): 22-28.

——— (1965a) Vnyeshnvaya Politika Yaponii Posle Vtoroi Mirovoi Voiny. Moscow: Mezhdunarodnoyye Otnosheniye.

——— (1965b) "Japan and the war in Viet Nam." International Affairs (November): 36-41.

——— (1972) Quoted in FBIS, USSR (February 22): C. 1-11.

Pravda (1972) April 27.

——— (1970) November.

——— (1964a) September 20.

——— (1964b) September 2.

SAEKI, K. (1972) "Ventures in Soviet diplomacy." Problems of Communism (May-June).

Seikai Orai (1972) "Beichu kyodo seimei no hamon." (April).

SEKINO, H. (1971) "Nihon no anzen to taisen mondai." Kokubo (June): 37-49.

——— (1970) "Kaiyo koku Nippon o do mamoru." Kokubo (March): 35-49.

SEMICHASTNOV, I. (1972a) Quoted in Current Digest of Soviet Press (March 29).
——— (1972b) Quoted in Izvestia (March 1).
SHERSHNEV, E. (1973) Peace in Asia. Tokyo: The Council on National Security Problems.
SHISHIKURA, J. (1972) "Soren no senryaku." Azia Kuotari (July): 82-93.
SLADKOVSKY, M. (1970) "Some lessons of the second world war in the Far East." International Affairs (October): 39-43.
SPAHR, W. (1973) "The Soviet views of Japan." pp. 170-192 in Y.C. Kim et al. Japan's Defense Policy. McLean, Va.: Research Analysis Corporation.
SPANDARYAN, V. (1971) Article in Pravda (October 20).
SUGIWARA, A. (1965) Gaiko no kangaekata. Tokyo: Kajima Kenkyujo.
SUGIYAMA, S. (1973) "Ryodo mondai wa donattaka." Sekai to Nippon (November 26).
——— (1972) "Diplomatic relations between Japan and the Soviet Union with particular emphasis on territorial questions." in Y.C. Kim (ed.) Japan in World Politics, Washington, D.C.: Institute for Asian Studies.
TAKANO, Y. (1962) "Hoppo ryodo no hori" in Y. Shien (ed.) Hoppo Ryodo no Chii. Tokyo: Nampo Doho Engo Kai.
Tass (1973) in FBIS, USSR (October 9).
TEPLINSKII, V. (1970) "Nekotorye aspekty global'noi strategii ssha." Mezhdunarodnaya Zhizn No. 3.
UEMURA, K. (1973) Article in Nihon Keizai Shimbun (July 26).
VASILYEV, V. (1969) "Japan rearms." New Times (June): 23-25.
YAMADA, H. (1972) "So-chu kankei no kako oyobi shorai o do miruka." Kokusai Jihyo (July): 12-15.
YAMAMOTO, H. (1951) "History of the Kuriles, Shikotan and the Habomai islands." Contemporary Japan (October-December).
YANO, T. (1973) "Soren no gaiko to Azia." Azia Kuotari (January-March): 105-113; 114-133.
ZAKHAROV, Y. (1972) "Japan on the threshold of 1972." International Affairs (February): 95-100.